# Spice Up
# Your Life

BY

## GAIL GRITTS

Independently Published
Printed in the USA


ISBN - 9798428640816

# INTRODUCTION

When life gets flat and you feel you aren't making any spiritual progress, it might be time to Spice Up Your Life. Using tried and true disciplines, these devotional readings encourage the believer to incorporate strong flavors and pleasing aromas into life for the benefit of peace, joy, and service.

# SPICE UP YOUR LIFE

Some people like spicy foods, some don't. I'm usually game to try anything once. I'd never tasted curry before I came to England. It has a very distinct flavor that, after a few goes, I learned to enjoy. And I fell in love with the flavor of Jamaican jerk chicken. Spices give food distinctive taste and typically point to the national origins of the dish.

A spiritual Christian has a distinct flavor described as a sweet-smelling savor or seasoned with salt. So, let's talk about spicing up our lives with spiritual spices that give us the beautiful aroma of strength and character.

Spirituality comes from experience, growth, and obedience to God's Word. No one can teach you to be spiritual. You cannot make yourself more spiritual, either. That is the work of the Holy Spirit. But you can open ourself to Biblical teaching and allow the Lord to develop your spirituality.

Years ago I learned that I am as spiritual today as my Christian experience has taken me. Each of us is on a different spiritual level, and that's okay. We are most likely strong in one area and weaker in another. And that's alright, too. Most of us have plenty of weak spots, but we also have a God who patiently works on repairing us! The secret to spirituality doesn't lie in who is ahead; it isn't a competition. The secret is a continual pattern of spiritual growth based on a personal relationship and chosen obedience to God's will.

The desire for instant satisfaction hinders spiritual growth. Spirituality does not come in a package. It is not a method to follow. It does not come overnight and will not come simply because you take on the suggestions we're going to consider. It is a life-long process of God working in you both "to will and to do of

His good pleasure" while He forms the image of Christ in your life. (Philippians 2:13) There is no quick fix!

Another thing that hinders spirituality is legalism-trying to live by laws or pious exercise. We cannot earn brownie points with God. He is not impressed with our strictness and rules but with the spirit by which we exercise obedience to His Word.

Thinking we will arrive at some acceptable spiritual plateau is also a falsehood. When we believe that, we fall into comparing ourselves with others. Just because we seem successful in one area does not mean we are spiritual. It is foolishness and pride that cause us to think we are better than someone else. We have no right to compare ourselves to others because we are all sinners. We are all on the path of sanctification.

Spirituality comes over time. In Romans 5:3-5 we read, "Knowing that tribulation worketh patience; And patience, experience; and experience, hope and hope maketh not ashamed." And James 1:3-4 reads, "Knowing this that the trying of your faith worketh patience but let patience have her perfect work, that ye may be perfect and entire, wanting nothing." Spirituality – sanctification – is a process. A beautiful process of God that spices up our lives.

It is not the result of our willpower. It isn't self-righteousness. It is a gift of God. And it is the fruit, or effect, of the working of the Spirit in our lives. To obtain any measure of spirituality, we must be willing to allow God to make changes.

The first spice we will consider is meditation. Let's begin with forming a definition. Meditation means, "To ponder; to revolve in the mind; to give something serious thought; to thoughtfully interpret." It is a biblical discipline taught in Psalm 119:97-104, Psalm 1:1-3, and Joshua 1:8. You might also want to look at Ephesians 5:19, Colossians 3:16, Philippians 4:8, and 1 Timothy 4:15.

Let's be sure we are on the same wavelength here. Eastern meditation, yoga, and secular meditation attempt to empty the mind, but

Christian meditation is filling the mind with the Word of God, pondering, revolving, and thoughtfully interpreting what God has said and who He is. We invite the Spirit to come and work in us, teaching, cleansing, comforting, and rebuking.

God can only work in us according to our willingness to surrender to Him. So, Christian meditation focuses on willing obedience and faithfulness to the Word as He reveals truth and gives direction.

We will face obstacles. Noises, distractions, interruptions, and the enemy's interference in our minds, life's demands, and even a lack of Bible knowledge can disrupt our attempts at mediation. But just because we find it hard doesn't mean it isn't a valuable discipline. There are beautiful scents and flavors in God's Word that you will only experience by meditation.

So how do you meditate? Well, it isn't worrying. It isn't trying to figure out a solution. It isn't rehearsing hurts or mulling things over. Let me share with you how I meditate. I find two main topics work best for me. One is Scripture, and the other is the attributes of God.

I usually meditate on the attributes of God when I take a prayer walk. When I am in nature, seeing the handiwork of God, He speaks to my heart about His character, ability, and provision...the list could go on and on. He reminds me of where He has met my need in the past and gives me hope for the future. As I think about His greatness, or His all-knowing, or His sovereignty in all things, He affirms them as true, and my heart bursts into praise and song. Meditating this way brings His presence very near and increases my faith and confidence. I love my prayer walks!

When I meditate using Scripture, I usually take a verse or short passage and work at memorizing it. I don't rush. I might meditate on that particular Scripture for days, weeks, even a month or more. It depends on what is happening in my life and what strength I need to draw from it.

For example, when I faced cancer, I meditated on 2 Timothy 4:17, "Notwithstanding the Lord stood with me; and strengthened me." I would take the word, notwithstanding, and put it into all sorts of scenarios. In every case, I found the Lord showed me how and where He had and would stand by me, and He did!

When I faced what I called the Year of the Impossible, I meditated on all the verses that spoke of God's ability like Mark 9:23, "All things are possible to him that believeth," and Luke 1:37, "With God, nothing shall be impossible" – and God showed up. It was an incredible year.

When we faced scary financial difficulties, I memorized and meditated on Matthew 6:19-7:11. Meditation helped me remember the precious promises of God. It increased my faith and helped me maintain perspective as I watched God bring us through.

As I meditated on these Scriptures at different times in my life, the truths and comforts I learned burrowed deep into my heart. They strengthened me and increased my faith, preparing me for similar events in the future. Even today, I can go back to my meditation spice and add richness and assurance – notwithstanding – right! Impossible? Not with God.

God knows meditation works and He even commands it. Psalm 1:2,3 – "But his delight is in the law of the Lord; and in his law doth he meditate day and night. And he shall be like a tree planted by the rivers of water, that bringeth forth his fruit in his season; his leaf also shall not wither; and whatsoever he doeth shall prosper." What a tremendous promise.

Joshua 1:8, "This book of the law shall not depart out of thy mouth, but thou shalt meditate therein day and night that thou mayest observe to do according to all that is written therein; for then thou shalt make thy way prosperous, and then thou shalt have good success." Meditation spices my life, and it will spice yours.

We can read all sorts of writers, listen to podcasts, and YouTube, sit under dozens of sermons, and serve the Lord in many ways, but without a personal, sincere time of feeding on the Word and meditation that results in obedience, we will not see the prosperous growth we desire in our spiritual lives, and we will not have the flavor or spice that influences others for Christ.

We will need a good measure of faith and flavor for the days ahead. So, getting into an attitude of meditation, taking time to look, pray over, think about, trust in, draw strength from, and apply what we learn, will better equip us for the journey. It will assure our prospering and make us a sweet-smelling savor to the Lord.

So, if you are lonely or hurt or feeling low or looking for answers, let me challenge you to begin setting aside at least five to ten minutes each day this week for nothing but thinking about either the attributes of God or a verse or two of Scripture. Psalm 1 is a great place to begin. Read it each day, then take one verse or a passage or even one word and ask the Lord to show you what He is saying. Open your heart and ears, and let the Spirit speak and spice up your life as you meditate.

**For thought:**

How many Scriptures do you know by heart?
How would your day change if you meditated instead of worrying?
Since what is in our heart comes out in our life, what influence would meditating have on your words and actions?

**Scriptures to consider:**

Psalm 1
Joshua 1:8
Psalm 119:59

# THE SPICE OF PRAYER

We have considered meditation—the beautiful, valuable spice that plants God's truth in our hearts and enables us to grow and understand more of who He is and what His Word says. Now, let's look at the quiet and personal spice of prayer.

George Muller was a man who knew the value of meditation and how it linked with prayer. He wrote, "It has pleased the Lord to teach me a truth, the benefit of which I have not lost for more than fourteen years. The point is this: I saw more clearly than ever that the first great and primary business to which I ought to attend every day was to have my soul happy in the Lord. The first thing to be concerned about was not how much I might serve the Lord, or how I might glorify the Lord, but how I might get my soul into a happy state, and how my inner man might be nourished.

I saw that the most important thing I had to do was to give myself to the reading of the Word of God – not prayer, but the Word of God. And here again, not the simple reading of the Word of God so that it only passes through my mind just as water runs through a pipe, but considering what I read, pondering over it, and applying it to my heart. To meditate on it, that thus my heart might be comforted, encouraged, warned, reproved, instructed. And that thus, by means of the Word of God, whilst meditating on it, my heart be brought into experimental communion with the Lord.

I began therefore to meditate on the New Testament from the beginning early in the morning. The first thing I did, after having asked in a few words the Lord's blessing upon His precious Word, was to begin to meditate on the Word of God, searching as it were into every verse to get blessing out of it.

When we pray, we speak to God. Now, prayer, in order to be continued for any length of time in any other than a formal manner, requires, generally speaking, a measure of strength or godly desires; and the season, therefore, when this exercise of the soul can be most effectively performed is after the inner man has been nourished by meditation on the Word of God, where we find our Father speaking to us, to encourage us, to comfort us, to instruct us, to humble us, or to reprove us.

By the blessing of God, I ascribe to this mode the help and strength which I have had from God to pass in peace through deeper trials, in various ways, than I had ever had before.

How different, when the soul is refreshed and made happy early in the morning, from what it is when, without spiritual preparation, the service, the trials, and the temptations of the day come upon me!" May 9, 1841

It may seem strange to use a long quote about meditating on God's Word into a lesson on prayer, but George Muller was known for his power in prayer, and this quote reveals the backdrop to his prayer life. He knew prayer alone was weak. Prayer must be coupled with meditation, God's Word, and our application of it to our lives.

Andrew Murray, another man who understood prayer, says, "How often the Christian, when he comes to pray, does his utmost to cultivate certain frames of mind which he thinks will be pleasing. He does not understand, or forgets, that life does not consist of so many loose pieces, of which now the one, then the other, can be taken up. Life is a whole, and the pious frame of the hour of prayer is judged of by God from the ordinary frame of the daily life of which the hour of prayer is but a small part. Not the feeling I call up, but the tone of my life during the day, is God's criterion of what I really am and desire."

Did you catch that? Our prayer life is not to be a random list of requests. It isn't a bunch of thoughts we throw together with whatever comes to our mind. It is the outflow of our everyday life. It is sweet communion with the One who already knows our requests, who understands the things happening around us, and who wants to bring comfort and assurance to our hearts – to make our soul happy in the Lord.

Matthew 6:6 gives another instruction, "But thou, when thou prayest, enter into thy closet and shut the door, pray to thy Father which is in secret; and thy Father which seeth in secret shall reward thee openly."

Shutting the door is to shut out things that would distract or cause interruption. It is to prioritize prayer while you talk to God Almighty - our Father, which art in heaven. Getting to our prayer closet and shutting the door is a daily challenge as life screams and competes for our attention. We begin with every intention of prayer and the phone rings, or we remember the clothes in the dryer, or our phone buzzes with a notification and we are easily side-tracked. To obey Matthew 6:6, we simply must learn how to shut the door and lay all these things aside for a set portion of time. We will come from our closet with a renewed zeal and find God gives us back the time spent with Him. At least, that has been my experience.

There are some things we can do to grow and increase our prayer life. First, we must be patient. James 1:3-4 reads, "Knowing this, that the trying of your faith worketh patience. But let patience have her perfect work, that ye may be perfect and entire, wanting nothing." And Hebrews 10:35- 36 says, "Cast not away, therefore, your confidence, which hath great recompense of reward. For ye have need of patience that, after ye have done the will of God, ye might receive the promise." A growing prayer life will not come quickly. You can't walk in and demand to be heard! You are building a relationship, and there is a lot of learning to be done, so be patient.

Also, you will find your prayer life ebbs back and forth. I have found this to be normal and frustrating! Some days I am so near the throne I could touch it, and other days I am far away down some long corridor, but I have found God always answers if I remain steadfast in prayer. Learning to pray is a life-long quest. That's what makes it such an important spice. It flavors everything.

I think of it as salt, and I believe it was C.H. Spurgeon who said he could always trace back anything he had done successfully to prayer – his prayer and the prayers of others praying for him.

Another thing about growing our prayer life is that it is directly proportionate to the strength of our faith. Romans 4:18-22 reminds us of Abraham's faith. He staggered not at the promise of God. Instead, he was fully persuaded that God would keep and perform His promise. We, too, must pray believing, not doubting, or wondering, but fully persuaded and solidly secure in the God of the promise.

Fearing our weakness will also inhibit a healthy prayer life. 2 Corinthians 12:9, 10 reminds us, "My grace is sufficient for thee; for my strength is made perfect in weakness…when I am weak, then am I strong." Sometimes, we imagine being a prayer warrior requires us to be some amazingly bold individual. The opposite is more likely! God looks for the contrite heart, the humble soul, and the submissive spirit. Oh, don't be confused. We are to come boldly before the throne, but that doesn't mean we come in our own strength – we come as the Spirit prays alongside us, we pray from our need, not our sufficiency. I don't know how often I have felt like I was stumbling in prayer to express my request only to see the Lord answer in astonishing ways.

Our prayer life will also increase when we realize we are not alone in prayer. Romans 8:26, 27 teaches that the Spirit helps – it means He prays alongside us. He interprets our thoughts and intercedes for us. Imagine, as you kneel in prayer, the Holy Spirit is right there beside you. All heaven is listening, and your prayers are being collecting in a celestial vial to be poured out as a precious incense before the throne of God. (Revelation 8:4)

One lesson on prayer is not adequate to exhaust this subject. I think of this spice as the most necessary, the most widely used, and probably the most powerful outside the Word of God alive in our hearts.

Let me recommend a few great books on prayer. One of my

favorites is <u>Life's Limitless Reach</u> by Jack Taylor. His book opened my eyes to prayer more than any I had read before. <u>The Kneeling Christian</u> is good. Its author is Unknown. <u>Fervent</u>, by Priscilla Shirer is a great blessing and challenge. <u>How to Listen to God</u> by Charles Stanley is also valuable, and I have recently enjoyed <u>The Circle Maker</u> by Mark Batterson.

Like salt, prayer flavors every area of our Christian growth, conflict resolution, decision making, family issues, and church issues. All things need prayer, and that's why we should learn to be prayer warriors. In 1 Thessalonians 5:17 we are admonished to pray without ceasing. So, what does prayer time look like to you?

Is it a short prayer before bedtime? Is it the prayer over your meal? Is it an early morning whisper before you rise? Is it talking to God through the day? Is it coming to God when you have a problem? It is setting aside a place and time devoted to nothing but prayer? Is it an awareness of God's presence so that the whisper of His name brings you before the throne?

Really, it is all these things. That's what it means to pray without ceasing - to have an attitude of prayer continually on your heart, ready to go the throne when life's demands get heavy, and even rejoicing there as you bring your praise and thanksgiving to God throughout the day. It is continual communion.

Prayer is like salt – it flavors every area. Without it, your Christian life is flat and tasteless. So, start setting aside five more minutes in your day. Add a five-minute prayer time after you have meditated on God's Word for five minutes. I would suggest you set yourself some alarms. One alarm for meditation, then, five minutes later, another for time to pray. Finally, add a third alarm to indicate your prayer time is complete. You'll be surprised at what happens in those simple ten minutes faithfully set aside for the Lord and how you will begin to look forward to this time when you shut the door and fellowship with your Saviour in prayer.

**For thought:**

What does your prayer life look like now?
How might it change if you gave the Lord five small minutes of serious prayer?
What is the most pressing prayer request on your heart today?


**Scriptures to consider:**

Romans 8:26, 27
Psalm 119:169,170
Psalm 4:4

# THE SPICE OF WAITING

I hope you have been practicing meditation and prayer. Let me assure you that alongside faithfully reading your Bible, these two spices are the basis of your growth, experience, and understanding in everything that forms your Christian life. Let me encourage you to keep making meditation and prayer a daily priority as we start looking at more spices.

A dear friend gave me a little book called <u>Waiting on God</u> by Andrew Murray. As I began reading it, the Lord assured me this was the next spice we needed to consider, for without it, all the others run the risk of being reduced to spiritual practice. So, let's talk about waiting.

Waiting is probably not a quality my family would credit to me. I am an A-type personality, and I prefer things done as soon as possible. I get annoyed waiting in a restaurant or standing in line, and I hate locked doors! But though waiting is not a part of my everyday qualities, I have learned much about waiting on God.

Andrew Murray writes, "If salvation indeed comes from God, and is entirely His work, just as our creation was, it follows as a matter of course, that our first and highest duty is to wait on Him to do that work as pleases Him." It reminds me of Philippians 1:6, one of my life's verses, "He that began a good work in you will perform it." God started the work in my life, and He will complete it. I must allow Him to work as He pleases and wait patiently and faithfully as He does, and so must you.

Galatians 3:3 also came to my mind. "Having begun in the Spirit, are ye now made perfect by the flesh?" In other words, if I was saved by faith in Christ alone, is my sanctification now accomplished by the works I do? No, it didn't. Just as I accepted

Christ's work for my salvation, I must also trust His working for my sanctification. It is a falsehood to believe we are responsible to create our own spirituality. It is a work of the Spirit.

Andrew Murray reminds us of another precious truth. "Man was not to have in himself a fountain of life, or strength or happiness. The ever-living and only living One was each moment to be the Communicator to him of all that he needed." Isn't that beautiful?

Through salvation, God places within us His Spirit. The Spirit does the work in my life and yours. We are totally inadequate to create anything of value. It is all of Him. This is the main secret in the spice of waiting. The work is being done in an unseen way, and the flavor is released as God sees fit. There is no way to rush the process.

In our current Christian society, we seem to believe our strength and happiness come from something we do – obey the Word, give, serve, etc. But that is directly opposite to what Scripture teaches, and to the spice of waiting. I know we want to see God at work in our lives and for Him to be answering our prayers, but He cannot work effectively and continuously if we do not let Him work His way. "We hinder Him by our self-effort, so that He cannot do what He would." We get in His way!

Galatians 3:3 starts with, "Are ye so foolish?" Well, are we? Do we think we come to Christ by faith and then serve Him through the flesh? Do we think our life, strength, and happiness are found in ourselves or in the outworking of our lives? The spice of waiting forces us to consider these questions because, without a biblical answer, we will fail to have the resource when we are called upon to wait.

We fall into this type of thinking because we are in a hurry to help things along. Imagine that! As if we could dictate to the Almighty. But we really seem to live as if we could. We even pray as if we could, and we make plans of our own before we consult and wait on His direction.

The pandemic caused us to do a lot of waiting, didn't it. A friend and I were talking the other day and concluded that there is nowhere in the world we could go to get away from this virus. God has all of us waiting. But remember, His timing is perfect. He does everything according to His purpose – even this time of pandemic.

I know waiting is hard, and sometimes, we might fear waiting on God will cause us to be left behind or feel ashamed. The psalmist must have had a similar concern when he prayed in Psalm 25 – "Let none that wait on thee be ashamed."

God intends that we wait, but it goes against our every grain, and we fret over the outcome. Some of us grow weary as the time of waiting feels so long. And some are fearful and don't know how to wait. Others get entangled in the effort of their prayers and think they have no time to wait continually on God; they need to be fixing the situation.

Andrew Murray writes, "There are times when waiting appears just losing time, but it is not so. Waiting, even in darkness, is unconscious advance, because it is God you have to do with, and He is working in you. God who calls you to wait on Him, sees your feeble efforts, and works in you. Your spiritual life is in no respect your own work; as little as you began it, can you continue it. It is God's Spirit who has begun the work in you of waiting upon God; He will enable you to wait continually."

Unconscious advance - what a concept. Even in our waiting, where we feel like nothing is happening, God is still at work. Have you experienced this?

Waiting is a learned skill. As we humble ourselves before God, we learn that we have nothing to hope in but His mercy. And actually, this is a beautiful place to be! We do not have any power within us to make things happen – and when we try – we usually make things more complicated. When we come to the end of ourselves and are forced to look up, we find God there waiting for us to do just that.

How much better would we be to look to Him first and wait on Him before we launch into new projects or ministries? To joyfully anticipate His working in the lives around us instead of trying to manipulate a result?

Another precious truth that came from my reading was Rev. Murray's thoughts on Psalm 33:18-22, ("The eye of the Lord is upon them that fear him.") "That eye sees the danger, and sees in tender love His trembling waiting child, and sees the moment when the heart is ripe for the blessing, and sees the way in which it is to come."

Isn't that precious? God knows we tremble. He knows we fear, but He also knows what will happen, how it will happen, and moves with perfect timing. We just need to trust Him.

Psalm 37:34 reads, "Wait on the Lord, and keep his way." Andrew Murray says, "We may be sure that God is never and nowhere to be found but in His way. And that there, by the soul who seeks and patiently waits, He is always most surely to be found." I want to be there, don't you? I want to be found waiting in the right way, doing the right thing, and trusting Him whate'er befall.

Here's another beautiful thought: "In every true prayer there are two hearts in exercise. The one is your heart, with its little, dark, human thoughts of what you need and what God can do. The other is God's great heart, with its infinite, divine purpose of blessing. What think you? To which of these two ought the larger place to be given in your approach to Him?" Good question. I'll leave you to answer that.

As we learn to wait before the Lord in prayer and meditation, we will begin seeing the smallness of our hearts, the darkness of our human thoughts, experience the immenseness of God's perspective, and feel the greatness of His love. Andrew Murray explains it this way, "But can we indeed enjoy it all the day? (God's love shining without ceasing) We can. And how can we? Let nature give us the answer. Those beautiful trees and flowers, with all this green grass, what do they do to keep the sun shining on them? They do nothing;

they simply bask in the sunshine, when it comes. The sun is millions of miles away, but over all that distance it comes, its own light and joy; the tiniest flower that lifts its little head upward is met by the same exuberance of light and blessing as flood the widest landscape. We have not to care for the light we need for our day's work. The sun cares, and provides and shines the light around us all the day. We simply count upon it, and receive it, and enjoy it.

The only difference between nature and grace is this – that what the trees and the flowers do unconsciously, as they drink in the blessing of the light, is to be with us a voluntary and a loving acceptance. Faith, simple faith in God's Word and love, is to be the opening of the eyes, the opening of the heart to receive and enjoy the unspeakable glory of His grace. And just as the trees, day by day, and month by month, stand and grow into beauty and fruitfulness, just welcoming whatever sunshine the sun may give, so it is the very highest exercise of our Christian life just to abide in the light of God, and let it and let Him, fill us with the life and the brightness it brings." (2 Corinthians 4:6 "For God, who commanded the light to shine out of darkness, hath shined in our hearts, to give the light of the knowledge of the glory of God in the face of Jesus Christ.")

You see, this spice of waiting is remarkably akin to acknowledging the power and presence of God in everything. It is a characteristic of humility and trust.

And what is the condition of God showing up? It is our waiting – waiting before Him in prayer, waiting for Him as we meditate on His beauty, greatness, and Word. Then watching God work all things according to the power of His will.

Let me encourage you to add this element to your meditation and prayer time. Create an interval of silence where you wait to hear from God. Add two minutes to your time, either between meditation and prayer or at the end. Stop planning, thinking, and worrying. Instead, sit quietly and listen to the Spirit. You might find God waiting for you there.

**For thought:**

Do you live life in a big hurry?
Are you trying to do spiritual works to justify yourself instead of relying on the work of the Spirit in your life?
Why do you struggle to schedule a time of waiting in your life?

**Scriptures to consider:**

Psalm 27:14
Psalm 40:1
Psalm 39:4-7

# THE SPICE OF WAITING AND WAITING

We are still talking about the spice of waiting. We learned that God is the one doing the work in our lives. Our part is to recognize His presence, His provision, His power, and allow Him to do the work – His way. I hope you added some quiet waiting time to your prayer and meditation moments. Putting these the spices of prayer, meditation, and waiting together will create a wonderful blend for your Christian life – better than a Pumpkin Spice Latte!

Let's start today by talking about what waiting looks like, or maybe it's better to start with what it isn't. It isn't seething, stressing, wailing on your bed, or fretting yourself into a frenzy. It isn't surmising or planning what you will say if this is said or what you will do if this is done. It isn't stubbornly sitting with your hands in your pockets or pouting because things aren't going your way.

Waiting is active, working alongside and cooperating with the Lord while you wait. Waiting is submissive, obeying instead of fighting against God. It is not complaining and living in fear. It is loving surrender to the will of God.

Waiting is hopeful, looking for the promise of His coming, anticipating His answer, and rejoicing ahead of time because faith assures you that He will show up.

Remember Isaiah 40:31? "They that wait upon the Lord shall renew their strength; they shall mount up with wings as eagles; they shall run, and not be weary; and they shall walk, and not faint." Do you know the tune to sing this verse? The lyrics end with, "Teach me, Lord. Teach me, Lord, to wait." So, waiting is a learned skill, and that word, shall, is the key. God shall, or will, renew us. We shall, or will, have victory. It is a promise for those who wait.

When God stirs up our nest, when we face disappointment, when our confidence is gone, and we fear and tremble, when waiting causes our strength to fail, and we begin feeling utterly weary and helpless, our Saviour spreads His strong wings for us to rest our weakness on and offers his everlasting strength. All He asks is that we "sink down in our weariness and wait on him." His strength will carry us. We can ride on the "wings of His omnipotence" as we choose to wait.

Okay, let's say that we understand God's ability, His abiding presence, and His supremacy in all things. That might be fine. You'd probably say, "Yes, Gail. I know that." But just because we accept these truths does not mean that we know how to live them out. We may still struggle with impatience and waiting.

Andrew Murray had an excellent thought on our predicament using Isaiah 30:18, "And therefore will the Lord wait, that he may be gracious unto you." He writes, "How is it, if He waits to be gracious, that even after I come and wait upon Him, He does not give the help I seek, but waits on longer and longer?"

Don't we feel like that sometimes? Like God has forgotten where we are? We hear ourselves calling out, "Hey, God! I'm waiting over here! Don't you care? Hurry up and answer my prayer, solve my problem. Show up. I'm tired of waiting!"

But Andrew Murray reminds us, "God is a wise husbandman, 'who waiteth for the precious fruit of the earth, and hath long patience for it.' He cannot gather the fruit till it is ripe. Waiting in the sunshine of His love is what will ripen the soul for His blessings. Waiting under the cloud of trial, that breaks in showers of blessing, is as needful. Be assured that if God waits longer than you wish, it is only to make the blessing doubly precious. God waited four thousand years, till the fullness of time, ere He sent His Son; our times are in His hands; He will make haste for our help and not delay one hour too long."

Did God wait four thousand years? Yes! God gave the promise of a Saviour in Genesis but didn't show up to complete the promise until the angel spoke to Mary in the book of Matthew! We won't have to wait that long, I'm sure!

But dear friend, I know some of you feel stuck, like it has been four thousand years with no vision for what your future holds. Rest assured; your Lord knows where you are. He sees you. He knows, and He cares. You can trust Him fully. When the time comes for your release, He will not delay one hour. Until then, draw closer to Him. Place yourself on His omnipotent wings and find the peace and comfort you need to continue waiting.

Here is another promise for you. Isaiah 49:23, "for they shall not be ashamed that wait for me." You will not be disappointed entrusting your life to Him. He is the Faithful God.

You can wait because waiting is a disposition that lies at the very root of our Christian life. It is one of the spices that reveals our trust. With so many examples in Scripture, how can we deny that truth?

Abraham waited, and his faith was counted for righteousness. He staggered not at the promise of God. And Sarah? She counted God faithful to His promise. They both waited a long time for that promised son. Joseph waited, and God made his dreams come true. Ruth waited, and God gave her a redeemer. David waited. God had already anointed him King, yet it was over fourteen years before he took the throne. Esther waited, and God used her to save her people. And **God** is still waiting – for the fullness of the Gentiles to come in! We are waiting collectively for the sound of the trumpet! They were not, and we will not be ashamed.

Let's go back to a Scripture we discussed previously. Psalm 27:13, 14 says, "I had fainted, unless I had believed to see the goodness of the Lord in the land of the living. Wait on the Lord; be of good courage, and he shall strengthen thine heart: wait, I say, on the Lord." Read carefully. The object of the waiting isn't the answer to prayer, and it isn't the solution to our problem. Instead, it is to see the goodness of the Lord.

As we wait to see God show up, He strengthens our hearts. Why? I think it is because the object of our waiting is much more satisfying than the resolution to our problem. The sight of our omnipotent, faithful Father and His goodness brings rejoicing to our hearts. Our situation pales by comparison. How much better when we lift our eyes off the temporary problems of this world and start looking up while we wait for His call.

When I grow weary in waiting, I come to Him in prayer pouring out my situation again and what does He do? He points me to new hope and gives me strength to wait a little longer. Each time my heart gets stronger. It's like lifting weights with God. I'm building spiritual muscle.

You will find great joy when you learn to rest in His arms and flow along with His plan. Eye hath not seen, nor ear heard, right? We are entrusting ourselves to the author and finisher of our faith.

A disposition of waiting reveals our commitment and is seen in a quiet assurance in God. It really is out of our control, anyway. So, what better place to rest our confidence than in an almighty, all-knowing, ever-loving God?

If you meditate on people in the Bible who waited, you can learn so much. Think of Elijah under the juniper tree. (1 Kings 19:5-8) God placed him there. Fed him, watered him. And what did Elijah do while he waited for his next assignment? He rested.

What do we usually do when we are in a waiting period? We struggle, feel guilty, start creating plans, cry, and whine. How much better it would be for us to rest in God's provision and simply enjoy the food and fellowship while we wait for our next assignment.

My husband and I have been meditating and talking about one word lately - prepared. God has all things prepared. There is nothing outside His preparation or left for Him to do. He has our needs, work, ministry, and future prepared already. When we take on this truth, it gives waiting more purpose.

Let's look at a few more scriptures together. Psalm 145:15, "The eyes of all wait upon thee; and thou givest them their meat in due season. Thou openest thine hand, and satisfies the desire of every living thing." He has everything prepared.

Psalm 39:7, "And now, Lord, what wait I for? My hope is in thee." Where else can you place your trust and not be disillusioned?

Isaiah 26:8, "Yea, in the way of thy judgments, O Lord, have we waited for thee; the desire of our soul is to thy name, and to the remembrance of thee." What are you waiting for? A miracle, a sign, or a Saviour?

Romans 8:19-28 tells us that the whole creation is waiting on God. Creation groans and waits.

Waiting then, Andrew Murray says, "links us, in unalterable dependence, to God Himself. We wait on Him to complete His promise. And it gives us the unbroken enjoyment of the goodness of God." Because we know He will answer. He is as good as His word.

Lamentations 3:26, "It is good that a man should both hope and quietly wait for the salvation of the Lord!" And that's what we are waiting for, right? To see the fruition of our salvation – to be with Him. So, we mustn't limit God by what we think can be expected. For with Him, all things are possible.

We are better to fix our eyes on God's very nature. He is the giver of life, and He cannot do otherwise than every moment work in His child and keep His promise. When we set God into the place of supremacy it makes waiting a more glorious task. It heightens our anticipation, strengthens our hearts, and brings glory to the Lord.

Dear friend, I have known moments of waiting as I prayed for a wayward child and saw God's answer. I have prayed for lost loved ones and seen them come to Christ. And I am still waiting. Unfortunately, not all my loved ones are saved. And I know what it is to wait to see how God would work in the impossible, which He has. I have at least two more impossible situations that repeatedly bring me to this truth of waiting. But I am waiting - waiting to see how God will solve the problems, how He will work things out His way—not mine.

And that's what I find so exciting about waiting. God always does more than I imagine. And He does it in a way where all the glory goes to Him, and I find myself thankful I waited. Meanwhile, I serve, trust, pray, rejoice, and anticipate His answer. You see, waiting is about looking for Him, waiting long for Him, and knowing in our heart that He will answer. He has already answered, it's all prepared, and He will show up!

So, today, if you are in a waiting period. Don't despair. God is right there beside you and waiting with you while He does a work in your life and in the lives of those around you. Cooperate with His work. Allow Him to reveal Himself and rest yourself in those everlasting arms and let Him strengthen your heart.

"He waits," Isaiah tells us, "That he might be gracious." Be thankful for that truth. God does things purposefully and consistently. Let's wait and see what He does!

**For thought:**

What are you waiting for?
Are you willing to trust God and stay faithful in the mean time?
God's goodness is there for you while you wait. Can you see Him blessing you?

**Scriptures to consider:**

Isaiah 40:31
Psalm 123:1, 2
Psalm 130:5, 6

# THE SPICE OF STUDY

Study doesn't sound much like a spice, does it. Ecclesiastes 12:12 even says, "much study is a weariness of the flesh." So why add this spice? Well, without study, you grow hungry. Study is how mature Christians feed themselves. They know the Bible is described as bread, meat, and milk, and they use it that way. Through the study of God's Word, they gain the sustenance needed to grow in Christ by adding Scriptural truth and understanding into their lives to face challenges and grow in the Lord.

The diet of daily devotional readings, five minutes of prayer, five minutes of meditation, and a couple of minutes waiting on God is insufficient. Even your one hour in church on Sunday morning or listening to a live stream is not enough to keep you spiritually healthy. You grow best when you learn to prepare meals for yourself. There are lots of ways to do that. I'm going to list for you several modes of study. If one captures your imagination, jot it down and give it a go.

You can study your Bible devotionally by reading and taking time to consider what you have read. Most people use this method. To do this, you read with the idea of looking to understand what is being said and how the characters are reacting. You look for promises to claim, instructions to follow, and sins to forsake; basically, see what the verses are saying to you personally. This method goes great with journaling as you keep a spiritual diary of what you have learned and, above all, how you have obeyed.

You can study for knowledge. This method has a variety of ways. For example, you can study chapters, paragraphs, or consider individual verses. With this mode, you are looking to increase your understanding, so look at the meaning of the words, the main subject, or thought, even try creating your own outline and take notes so you can look up any questions that come. You dig in and do research to gain knowledge – studying to show yourself approved.

You can study by book. There are different ways to approach this as well. You can do what they call Inductive study – taking the details and drawing conclusions or principles from the book. Most pastors create their sermons using this method. Synthetic – reading to get the general impression and purpose without focusing on the detail – looking for the flavor of the book. Or Historical – reading to put the book into the history of a nation or person in a particular timeline. For example, when you read the Minor Prophets, and you put each book into the timeline of the Children of Israel. That way, you see what happened when they wrote and who they were writing to. This improves your overall understanding of the framework of the Old Testament.

Some people study by biography. They choose a Bible character, read their story in God's Word, and then read a few other books written about that character. When you study by biography, you look to see the principles by which the individual lived, their decisions, the outcome of their choices, and draw some conclusions for yourself. You also look for Scriptures that corroborate what you have found. Remember, no matter what method you use, always double-check your conclusions by Scripture!

I like to study by topics. I choose a topic, like Bible prayers, promises, songs, marriage, tithing, etc., and using a resource book, concordance, and topical Bible, I look at all the verses and passages related to that topic. This is a great way to come to understand broader teachings. When I was a young Christian this was my favorite way to learn. I had loads of questions, so a topical Bible and a concordance were my best two resources to find the answers I needed in Scripture.

Over the last few years, my favorite way to study is by words. I get a topical Bible, look at one word, and research out all the verses using that particular word. Then, I go to the concordance and see that I understand the original meaning of the verse. Then, I read a few commentators. I always have liked Matthew Henry, Albert Barnes, and W.E. Vine. But maybe you have some others you prefer. See what they say, make some notes, and let the Lord feed you.

Some books of the Bible have recurring words. For example, Philippians uses the word joy. John uses the word believe, and Hebrews the word better. And another fun one is to look at the word all in the book of Colossians. The book of Ezekiel has a phrase that is repeated – "ye shall know that I am the Lord." But whatever word you choose to study, or whatever method you enjoy, the real secret to study is application, application, application.

Study is like a marinade or a spice rub. It needs time to sink in. So, don't rush. Instead, take as long as you need and get all you can out of your study. Let it become something you long for - a flavor that lingers.

Nowadays, my study takes a few direct paths. I might be studying so I can write or teach, and I gain a lot from that, but study done to give out is not the type we are talking about. You need study that feeds you personally.

And another way I study is to find answers for people. Counseling demands I investigate, and I benefit from that too, but again, it is not a private meal for personal nourishment. It is more like mixing up the batter for a cake. Hopefully, I'm putting all the ingredients together to produce a functional finished product I can give away.

I'm finding that studying according to where the Spirit points my attention is most beneficial for me lately. It's more like the devotional type of study. Let me give you an example. Last week I started 2 Corinthians in my daily reading. Things started popping up and speaking to my heart. The Word was meeting me at my need, pointing out things for me to grasp, and challenging me to look deeper. I'm going to share with you almost directly from my journal from that day.

I wrote, "Began 2 Corinthians today, and loads of things pop up to be studied. (I listed these verses and made a few short notes.)

Verse 8 – pressed out of measure. (I was feeling pressured that day, so this verse helped me remember that God knows I face pressure.)

Verse 9 – not trust in ourselves – reminds me of Luke 18:11 where the Pharisee "prayed thus with himself."

Verse 12 – simplicity – this is one of the upcoming spices, need to make note and study more on this word.

Verses 21-22 - Christ establishes, God anoints, and the Holy Spirit seals.

Verse 24 – we are "helpers of your joy." I think this is my study for the day!"

Following this entry, I pulled out a few resource books and then recorded what I found from two of the noted phrases.

Verse 9 had brought the idea of not trusting in ourselves. I studied the phrase, "trusted in themselves," and it reminded me of the phrase "prayed thus with himself" I caught a few weeks prior as I read through Luke 18:11, and I had meditated and prayed about that phrase for several weeks. Today, I needed to study it out. What did it mean that the Pharisee prayed with himself? Was I ever guilty of praying with myself – talking to myself instead of God? Was that what the phrase meant? I was concerned that I could think I was praying and just be talking to myself.

Here's what I recorded in my journal after a bit of study. "So, Luke 18:11, Matthew Henry says, "He was wholly intent upon himself, had nothing in his eye but self, not God's glory. Here is not one word of prayer in all he saith, He went up to the temple to pray, but forgot his errand. He thought he had need of nothing, no, not the favour and grace of God, which, it would seem he did not think worth asking."

I write – "And did God hear his words? Obviously! For God gives the judgment of the two prayers – humility justifies. Pride is abased. As Matthew Henry puts it, pride – makes one "rivals with God."

My devotional study on the phrase "prayed with himself" was prompted by the phrase in 2 Corinthians, "Not to trust in ourselves." Study helps me link ideas together. When 2 Corinthians tells me not to trust in ourselves, I now have another outlook – the outlook of pride in prayer. It brings a deeper flavor and richer spice into my meal.

How will I apply this to my life? What did I learn? I need to consider my attitude in prayer. I can't come to God with pride in myself and expect Him to be honored. I don't want to be a rival with God because I trust in myself or get prideful.

My journal also records thought on the phrase, "helpers of your joy," in 2 Corinthians 1:24. I remember the brightness of this phrase. It would make a great t-shirt! Helpers of Your Joy!

After some more study I wrote, "We are servants – ministering light and love to those in our care. Helping them to find the same joy we know in Christ and the gifts of Philippians 2:1-2 – consolation, comfort, fellowship, so that Philippians 2:17-18 – we might rejoice together."

Study of God's Word weaves ideas together. The Spirit can use one word or phrase to give us the taste of another morsel. We get a whole meal, and the beauty of it draws us back for more!

And then, there is a little prayer I recorded. "Lord, may I be a helper of joy. Use me to encourage, to plant hope, to bring closer to your love and fellowship those who are hurting and astray."

These two little records of study still rejoice my heart. And my journal is full of things like this. Every time I go back and read, I am reminded of the wonderful meals I have enjoyed while studying in God's word, looking for treasure, and applying the spice of richer truth to my life.

So, let me encourage you. Start with a study that interests you. Get yourself a topical Bible. You can even access them for free online. Learn to use a concordance, like Strong's Exhaustive Concordance, so you can double-check the original meanings and get a commentary. I learned from Matthew Henry. And you can access his commentary online as well. With those three tools, you can learn so much and consistently feed yourself some flavor-able meals!

Why else should you do this? Because it is a command of God. 2 Timothy 2:15 "Study to shew thyself approved unto God, a workman that needeth not to be ashamed, rightly dividing the word of truth."

So, while you meditate, pray, and wait, pick up your Bible and a few resources and feed yourself. Learn something new each day. Study!

**For thought:**

What is your favorite way to study your Bible?
Have you ever gone further than simply reading? Why not?
Do you feed yourself or are you reliant on the Sunday sermon?


**Scriptures to consider:**

Psalm 119:9-12
2 Timothy 3:16, 17
Hebrews 2:1

# THE SPICE OF SIMPLICITY

What do you think of when you hear the word simplicity? Something easy to do? Having less stuff? Living like Amish people? Being simple-minded?

I thought it meant living modestly or somewhat minimalist. But after studying it out, I found God's Word holds a much more intense aroma for this spice.

I found two interpretations of the meaning. Some commentators said the word means without duplicity—single-mindedness, sincere, plain-hearted, or straightforward. And others interpreted it as liberality, meaning generous giving, bountifulness. Neither of those was what I had in my mind. So, when authors can't agree, I go to Scripture and rub in some more of that spice of study! Here's what I found.

The word is translated as simplicity only two times in the Old Testament. In 2 Samuel 15:11, a group of men followed Absalom, and "they went in their simplicity," meaning their innocence or integrity. And in Proverbs 1:22, "how long, ye simple ones, will ye love simplicity." Here it means to be naïve, easily deceived, or persuaded.

The word simplicity is used only three times in the New Testament. According to Strong's Concordance, it means "the moral quality of honesty expressed by singleness of purpose, generosity, and the giving of things in a manner that shows liberality." It doesn't sound anything like how we use the word today.

When Romans 12:8 says, "He that giveth, let him do it with

simplicity." It means we should give generously and with an honest purpose.

When 2 Corinthians 1:12 tells us our testimony is to be "In simplicity and godly sincerity," it indicates we are to have a testimony that shows our singleness of purpose and generosity.

And in 2 Corinthians 11:3, we are not to be "corrupted from the simplicity that is in Christ." In other words, we are not to move away from the beautiful example of Christ's sacrificial giving – the simplicity of the Gospel lies in His generosity and singleness of purpose - the salvation of our souls.

So, let's talk about the two sides of the definition –singleness of purpose and generosity. A perfect place to start is Matthew 6:24. "No man can serve two masters: for either he will hate the one, and love the other; or else he will hold to the one, and despise the other. Ye cannot serve God and mammon." We must make a purposeful choice. We can even look at Joshua 24:15, "Choose you this day whom you will serve…as for me and my house we will serve the Lord." Or Colossians 1:18, "In all things he might have the pre-eminence. Or Paul's attitude in Philippians 3:13 – "this one thing I do." He had a focused purpose, and we are to have the same.

The spice of simplicity gives forth the fragrance of dedication to God. It has one purpose – to glorify Him by following and letting Him be the most essential thing in life. And with everything in its being, it will give to that end.

Wow! Now that is a far cry from what I thought the word meant. How about you?

In Matthew 6, the Lord instructions our attitude toward His ability to provide and comes back to this central theme of singleness of purpose in verse 33 by saying, "But seek ye first the kingdom of God, and his righteousness; and all these things shall be added unto you."

This singleness of purpose gives us three inner attitudes. We will receive all that comes as a gift from God. James 1:17 tells us "Every good gift and every perfect gift cometh from above." This gives us perspective. Then, we accept that things are temporal. Proverbs 23:4,5 tells us riches fly away, so don't set your heart on them. Instead, we are instructed to lay up treasure in heaven because the earthly treasure is temporary and can be lost. (Matthew 6:19-20) This teaches us how to apportion value. Finally, singleness of purpose opens our hearts to make what we have available to others in the service of God. Here are three examples. 1 Chronicles 29:9 – the people gave willingly. James 2:15, 16 – if you see a brother in need, you should meet his need, not just say God bless you and do nothing to help. And in Acts 4:34-35, the New Testament church distributed to the needs of each other, liberally, so no one had need.

That brings us to the liberality, generosity side of simplicity. Our need to hang on to stuff, hoard, or be greedy goes against our purpose. We are to exemplify the generosity of our Lord. He gave, and so should we. Giving is the simplicity of the Gospel. Albert Barnes says, "craft, artful plans, and deep-laid schemes of deceit belong to the world: simplicity of aim and purpose are the true characteristics of a real Christian." And they are shown by how we give to others.

A mindset of simplicity sets possessions in their proper order; it frees us to receive God's gifts and makes us willing to share. And a life of joyful unconcern for possessions frees us from anxiety and protects us from greed, which brings a snare according to 1 Timothy 6:9. Simplicity is an inward focus of purpose that brings freedom to enjoy our possessions and not pine for what we do not have.

I'd never really thought about the link between anxiety and simplicity, but as I meditated, I began to put more things together. The more stuff we have, the more we must dust, protect, and store. The larger our income, the more we spend on bigger houses, fancier cars, and newer gadgets.

As a result, we go further and further into debt, which goes against simplicity. The more we possess, the more anxiety we face because we fear losing it. We get protective and selfish. We are never content as we constantly upgrade. Constant upgrading deceives us into believing we will be satisfied with the next gadget, but we are failing to recognize the unseen pressure we place on our lives. Why? Because our hearts are not living with a focus on seeking God first. We are seeking stuff, and it never satisfies.

Satan would have us believe God is cheating us if we don't have as much as everyone else. He tries to convince us we are missing out on all the good stuff. He uses the same deceptive practices on us as he used on Eve. Namely: The lust of the flesh, the lust of the eyes, and the pride of life. (I John 2:15,17 James 4:1-5; 5:1-6 Phil. 3:7, 8.)

Our current culture lacks the inward attitude or purpose and outward lifestyle of generosity. Instead, we seem trapped in a maze of things pulling our attention, which gets our focus off God.

I believe we've had time to take a cold, hard look at our accumulation and culture during the pandemic. If we haven't, now is a good time! Hopefully, we've decided what's essential. What we truly desired and missed were friendships and fellowship. Not stuff, right?

And, if we are praying, meditating, waiting on God, and studying, using all these spices, we will be aware of the enemy's devices and the attitude of this world. We will recognize that temptation to take on more than we can afford, or more than we can do, and we will be less likely to fall for things like trying to impress others by what we have or what we can do, the accumulation of stuff to no purpose, and even the need to please others or unduly impress them. These attitudes go against the spice of simplicity. They create drama and anxiety because we are grasping for temporal things. As a result, we become unstable, double-minded, discontent, and selfish.

How can we avoid this? By focusing in one direction, seeking the

Lord and His righteousness, not our own. Focus is a balancer in all our decisions. It makes things much simpler!

Let's talk a bit more about this generosity side of simplicity. Giving isn't solely about money and things. We give our time, our love, and our effort to the needs of others. We seek to look out for the welfare of those around us. That is also generosity. It is the picture of what Christ would have us do.

When we look at the example of the New Testament church, we see them having fellowship, breaking bread, and teaching with no gimmicks or extravagant church programs. They were known by their love for one another and the example of Christ they portrayed. Love and generosity flowed from them. They cared for each other on purpose - sacrificially and liberally. James 1:27 says, "Pure religion and undefiled before God and the Father is this, To visit the fatherless and widows in their affliction, and to keep himself unspotted from the world." It sounds so simple. Our love is to flow to those in need, generously and liberally, and prompt us to keep our focus on purity in Christ – one focus.

Study Matthew 6:24-33 for yourself or read it through each day for this passage is the central point for simplicity. Memorize as much as you can, especially Matthew 6:33. Meditate, pray, and wait on God to reveal more about simplicity.

Then, take time to evaluate what to add to your life, amend, and leave behind. Pare things down and make life more manageable. Let life become less complicated, less contaminated, and more focused on seeking God. Look to see where your simplicity and desire to give can flow to others in a generous and loving manner that honors the Lord.

Strive to live a simple life with one goal – to seek God and His righteousness, then, God promises, all these other things will be added to you. How simple is that?

**For thought:**

Are you often overcome by anxiety due to all the stuff you have to manage?
Where is generosity active in your life?
What is your life's main purpose?

**Scriptures to consider:**

2 Corinthians 4:18
Hebrews 13:16
Luke 6:38

# THE SPICE OF SOLITUDE

Be Still My Heart

Our spice for today is the spice of stillness or solitude. This study has brought me a certain amount of unsettled emotion. Either the enemy does not want me sharing this spice's secrets, or God wants to be sure I understand more of what it means. It's definitely been a study using meditation, prayer, and inner searching.

The spice of solitude makes some people very happy because they love time alone. Others really struggle to enjoy this flavor. They greatly prefer constant company and activity.

Quiet hearts are rare these days, aren't they? Finding stillness is a challenge because of the subconscious pressure we feel during this pandemic, the uncertainty of our political and economic futures, the buzz of social media, and the volatile emotions of people around us.

I'm finding that true, aren't you? So, as we look at this spice, I want you to know that I, too, struggle at times to maintain the peace of heart I need in this storm. But my weakness or humanness does not cancel the instruction of Scripture or the necessity of obedience to what God says is best.

I find inner stillness is most usually associated with where I place my trust and the quality of my alone time with God. I know inner preparation is necessary for outward service.

Oswald Chambers says, "Strength lies in soaking before God. You have no idea of where God is going to engineer your circumstances, no knowledge of what strain is going to be put on you either at home or abroad, and if you waste your time in overactive energies instead of getting into soak on the great fundamental truths of God's Redemption, you will snap when the strain comes; but if this time of soaking before God is being spent in getting rooted and grounded in God, you will remain true to Him whatever happens."

I like the idea of soaking before God. To rest and take in all He is, to stop and contemplate, to soak up His Word, and to apply the balm of the Spirit gives strength to my life. So let's begin with a definition and some insights from Scripture.

Solitude is an inward attitude not dependent on our circumstances. It isn't loneliness because loneliness is inner emptiness, but solitude is inner fulfillment. Inner solitude and silence set us free from loneliness and fear because we understand we aren't alone.

The verse most of us know is Psalm 46:10, "Be still and know that I am God." God is there with us in our solitude—in our stillness. We aren't alone; we are drawing aside to Him.

Wayne Muller calls it a "portable sanctuary" of the heart. We can go there at any time. As Psalm 4:4 says, we commune with the Lord, even while we are in bed. We are alone, but not alone because the Lord is always with us.

Jesus lived with an inward solitude – a portable sanctuary. We see Him drawing aside, departing into a desert place, a wilderness, or sometimes a mountain apart from the disciples and the crowds clambering for His attention by seeking out in a solitary place to pray and meet with God. Each time He withdrew, it was to draw strength for continued ministry. We would be wise to take His example by seeking out the recreating stillness of solitude where we can pray, reflect, and regroup.

For those who enjoy solitude, it is like coming home to the smell of something in the oven. That inviting aroma leads you straight to the kitchen where food is waiting. Solitude does this. It draws us back, warms our hearts, and whets our appetite for more of the Word and fellowship with Christ. It's a very personal communion.

But some people fear being alone, which drives them to noise and crowds. They allow fear and sadness to speed up their lives. Terrified of the grief and pain in life and trying to avoid the harsh and piercing realities, they move faster and faster, attempting to escape how sad they feel, the loss they have experienced, the broken dreams, and disappointments of life. If they stop, for even a moment, fear overtakes them.

They fear because they may have unaddressed issues or things to hide or feel shame, but the eyes of God are open to our every thought, idea, and motive. Psalm 139 teaches we cannot hide from God, and no amount of feverish activity can change that fact.

In your lone moments and your sleeping hours, God is there beside you because He loves you. How much better to place yourself before Him as David did in Psalm 139:23, 24 "Search me, O God, and know my heart: try me, and know my thoughts."

God knows them already, but He waits for your invitation. Allow Him to show you what He sees, what He wants to help you overcome. Nothing can separate you from His love. Romans 8:38-39, "neither death nor life...height or depth...or any creature...can separate us from the love of God." It is safe to invite God into your life.

When you are open before God, holding nothing back, you arrive at the station of His love and acceptance. There is no fear because His perfect love casts out fear. (1 John 4:18)

Hebrews 4:13 tells us, "All things are open to the eyes of him with whom we have to do, and that moves us to verse 16 where God says, "Come boldly to find grace to help in time of need." God calls you to the throne, not to scold you, but to give you grace, help you, heal you, bind your wounds, and repair your heart. He wants to spend time with you. He stands at the door of your heart, knocking. Will you let Him in?

If you fear solitude, you need to look to the reason why. Use Open

Exposure as taught in James 5:16. Find that friend who will listen and pray with you. Confess your fault, pray together, and ask the Lord to heal you.

And if it isn't fear that overtakes people, sometimes it is that sound of emptiness, nothingness, or feelings of unworthiness. They believe nothing can fill their void, so it looks like a monster, a horrible, insatiable monster coming to eat them alive. And what do they do?

First, they try to keep busy by filling their calendar with events, tasks, and errands while they act happy. Then, trying to hold it all together, they eat, spend, drive fast, drink, take drugs – anything to fill the empty hole in their lives. "But this emptiness," Wayne Muller says, "has nothing at all to do with our value or our worth. All life has emptiness at its core."

God wants to fill that empty part. And it is in solitude and communion where He meets us.

Wayne Muller continues, "Solitude is the quiet hollow reed through which the wind of God blows and makes the music that is our life. Without that emptiness, we are clogged and unable to give birth to music, love, or kindness. All creation springs from emptiness."

God loves empty spaces! He does his best work there. Look at all He did with the creation from the earth without form and void. And He can do wonderful things with your emptiness, too! So, there is no reason to fear or to run or to hide. God loves you right where you are, so STOP.

When I feel empty, my mind goes to Romans 7:18 – "For I know that in me, that is in my flesh dwelleth no good thing." I must agree—no sense arguing my worthiness. I have no worthiness of my own.

Verse 24 asks the question for me, "O wretched man that I am, who shall deliver me from this body of death?" And verse 25 answers, "I thank God through Jesus Christ our Lord." My worth is in Him. He fills my emptiness and makes me complete in Him. He can do the same for you.

Solitude opens dialogue with God. Think with me about these examples. Elijah was alone in the cave, and God talked with him. Isaiah saw God high and lifted up. What a time of fellowship he had before God. Elijah recognized his emptiness, but it brought awe and humility instead of fear. Paul talks about a sweet time of aloneness with God as he was caught up in the third heaven and saw unspeakable things. Hagar languished alone in the desert, but God met her there with tender care. All of them experienced a visit from God in their time of solitude.

When we pray, we shut the door. We get alone. We wait and meditate. Each of these spices involves solitude, and we come out singing, "And He walks with me and he talks with me, and he tells me I am his own, and the joy we share as we tarry there, none other has ever known."

We have a hard time hearing God when we are going ninety miles per hour. He needs us to stop so we can listen. So, solitude requires time, and there is nothing so beautiful or precious as time alone with your Saviour.

Just as some plants will not bear fruit without lying dormant, we, too, need times of respite. It is a spiritual and biological necessity. A lack of rest produces confusion, poor health, and erodes our inner man. But when we disconnect from cyberspace, from our frenzied consumption of media, and our hectic, demanding lifestyle, we can draw ourselves back to the flavor of God's Word and the fellowship and love we so desperately desire.

Solitude helps us create simplicity. It gets our purpose realigned and gives us more generosity and energy to give out again.

As a young mother with five children under the age of seven, I came to times when I needed just ten minutes to regroup. I'd tell them, "Mommy is closed." And I'd go to the bedroom and shut the door, pray, lay down, or sit in the dark for a few minutes while I took a deep breath before opening the door again. There I would find loving little eyes waiting for my return. And I'd have the energy and calmness to carry on with the day.

Jesus' example shows us the benefits of quiet time alone with God and solitude. He walked through life assured of God's control. Jesus never doubted but moved serenely with a purpose, in love toward friend and foe, free from worry because He knew God was doing the caring. Jesus knew his mission was to do the Father's will, and He did it with simplicity, aim, and liberality. Solitude helped Him stay on track. It will help you, too.

So how can you develop this spice in your life?

Well, start by setting aside time. We have talked about prayer, meditation, study, and waiting. Like solitude, all of these take time, and we can practice them throughout the day.

If you can set aside even one hour a week to withdraw to reorient your life goals and priorities or open your heart to the Lord's examination, then do it. That is a great way to start. Maybe choose a day to go to bed an hour earlier; that works for me, especially on a Saturday in prep for Sunday.

Or, I find I must catch times when everyone else is out of the house. I relish those times. I got one precious hour this week to do that! I make that time special and talk aloud to the Lord in prayer. I sing, and I talk things through with the Lord. Sometimes I sit quietly, allowing my heart and mind to focus and meditate on God's goodness, His love for me, or how He has worked in my life.

Being still and knowing that He is God creates a beautiful solitude that carries me for days. So, take advantage of the "little solitudes" that fill your day like while you are washing dishes, taking a walk, folding laundry, driving to or from work, or waiting for an appointment. Draw your heart and mind aside. Don't plan or worry. Use that time to sit your soul at the Saviour's feet.

Find, or develop a "quiet place" of your own, if you haven't done that already. Emily Barnes talks about having your Bible, a pen and notebook, a devotional, and some tissues in a basket that you can grab at any moment and have time alone with the Lord.

I used to have a basket like that. It kept my things together so I could take them outside with me or into a different room when I needed solitude and time to focus on the Lord.

What will solitude do for you? Well, look at the example of Jesus again. After each time of solitude, there came a time of ministry and increased compassion for others. Do you need that? More compassion for others. Solitude works. Even ten minutes of complete quiet can re-initiate your patience and endurance.

Solitude also increases your communion with God and gives you spiritual strength. Isaiah 30:15 says, "In returning and rest shall ye be saved; in quietness and in confidence shall be your strength." Aren't those beautiful things? – quietness, confidence, returning, and rest.

God knows we need a time of quiet rest, and He invites us to do so. Matthew 10:28 is the verse that keeps popping up in front of me. "Come unto me, all ye that labour and are heavy laden, and I will give you rest. Take my yoke upon you, and learn of me; for I am meek and lowly in heart; and ye shall find rest unto your souls. For my yoke is easy and my burden is light."

God has often used this verse to remind me of the need for solitude, rest, and realignment that can only come from Him.

So, I challenge you to try solitude. Take time alone with God on purpose. Seek to develop an inner sanctuary in your heart and let Him meet you there as you still your heart before Him. Don't be afraid. He comes with a meek and lowly spirit in love for your soul.

I think you will find solitude draws you back to God, warms your hearts, and makes you hungry for more.

**For thought:**

Have you developed an inner, portable sanctuary in your heart?
Do you fear being alone?
What benefits do you experience in times of personal solitude?

**Scriptures to consider:**

Psalm 94:19
Psalm 32:7
Proverbs 18:10

# THE SPICE OF CONTENTMENT

Do You Smell Smoke?

Jeremiah Burroughs defines contentment as "that sweet, inward, quiet, gracious frame of spirit, which freely submits to and delights in God's wise and fatherly disposal in every condition." Take time to read that again and let it soak in a while. As we come to think about contentment, I want to try and help us see it from two perspectives - the excellence of this spice and then the stinky misuse called discontentment.

I find contentment probably another of those most valuable spices on my spiritual spice rack. It's right up there with prayer and meditation because its flavor is so distinct. Contentment lets me see beauty. It brings rest to my soul and thankfulness to my heart. I see potential, God's loving hand, and experience hope and joy when I am content. When I am not content, I murmur, get angry, argue, and have all sorts of disagreeable tendencies.

But before we talk about all these aggravations, let's smell the beautiful fragrance of this spice. We can draw these flavors from Burroughs' definition, "Contentment is that sweet, inward, quiet, gracious frame of spirit, which freely submits to and delights in God's wise and fatherly disposal in every condition."

When we're content, we give God the worship He is due by freely submitting and delighting in Him. When we're content, we have strength in the face of hardship, beauty in the middle of trials, and we learn to exercise hope, wisdom, patience, and many other graces. When we're content, we serve others and our Lord with a peaceable and steadfast heart because our inward spirit is sweet, quiet, and gracious. When we're content, we enjoy what we have, gratefully recognizing God's provision, and with His abiding light in our eyes we see things positively, hopefully, and with a different aspect. And, when we're content, we enjoy things that we do not possess, and we draw nearer God himself because He is the source of contentment, peace, and rest.

Doesn't that smell wonderful? It's a great place to be!

But without contentment, we are very different creatures. We live with a murmuring spirit and an inner aggravation that makes us unserviceable for the cause of Christ and troublesome to others. Joy and hope disappear and we are left with an inner anxiety and bitterness that pours out in our words and expressions.

I'm hoping your nose starts to smell the difference. It's one thing to talk about the sweet, quiet, and gracious frame Christians should exhibit, but it is another to be honest about the murmuring, aggravating, and troublesome spirit that inhabits our lives and service.

Let's start with why a murmuring spirit is so detrimental. Jeremiah Burroughs gives us thirteen reasons. You will need to use the spice of study to take this all in, so read slowly and measure yourself as you go.

1. Murmuring reveals the corruption of our soul. It shows how dirty we are and must be purged from within by repentance.
2. Murmuring is connected with the ungodly in Scripture – Jude 14-16
3. God accounts murmuring as rebellion. Just look at the murmuring of the children of Israel. Burroughs says, "murmuring is smoke." It shows there is a burning problem somewhere. I've found that very accurate. In myself and others, it smells like smoke.
4. Murmuring is contrary to the grace and work of God. Murmurers avoid seeing their sin. They want to cling to their complaints and refuse to yield to the King. They do not have a submissive spirit.
5. Murmuring and discontent are, as Burroughs puts it, "exceedingly below a Christian." He says it is below us because of our stand in Christ; we a part of the body, co-

heir with Christ. We are called to live higher, with dignity as children of light and not with a childish, selfish spirit attached to the world and longing for the things of the world. God expects more of us. He expects us to rely on His promises and be a Christian of faith, as seen in Hebrews 11. Murmuring and discontent should be below us.

6. Murmuring undoes your prayers. Burroughs says, "Prayer is yielding, murmuring is demanding."

7. Murmuring and discontent have the following woeful effects.

   a. You lose a great deal of time when you murmur. You can't meditate on God, but you can fret and complain for hours? Something is wrong!

   b. It unfits you for duty. Who wants to work with a complainer?

   c. You find wicked thoughts rising in your heart and spirit.

   d. Unthankfulness reigns.

   e. And it causes a shifting in your spirit – it changes you, and everyone around you smells it!

8. It takes away the present comfort of what you have and breeds unthankfulness. It does not produce what you are wanting, but rather it creates foolish attitudes and shame by the words and actions it manufactures. It eats out the good and sweetness of mercy, leaving you hollow, and makes the affliction/complaint worse by fueling a prideful heart that will not yield to love and mercy.

Burroughs isn't finished!

9. There is danger in discontent, for it provokes the wrath of God. Look at Korah. The children of Israel saw God's displeasure and His judgment on the complaining hearts. Don't know that story? Read Numbers 16:1-33.

10. It is cursed of God because it is the opposite of serving with joy. Take time to look at Deuteronomy 28:45-47. God is serious about our attitude in service. He wants joyful servants, not complainers.

11. Murmuring and discontent are Satan's influence. He promotes discontentment and wants us to be striving with our Maker.
12. Murmuring and discontent will last all your life if you choose it – it is a choice! Sadly, I've known people like this. Their every response is negative. They look for the worst and are rarely happy with any good that comes their way. How sad.
13. God may withdraw. If we are not humbled by our sin of murmuring and repent of it, we will but return to it over and over, tempting God and frustrating the Spirit.

Can you smell this off-putting odor of discontentment? Let's squeeze some more out. Maybe even get it out of our system today. Indeed, to murmur and be discontent when we enjoy an abundance of mercy is the vilest of sins. So, why do we continue murmuring?

We murmur over small things out of our reach, as Ahab did. He couldn't have the garden he wanted, so he cried on his bed. He didn't care what happened to the garden's owner as long as he got what he wanted. You can read this story in 1 Kings 21:1-16.

How selfish are murmuring and discontent? For Ahab, his discontent led to murder.

We murmur out of jealousy or because we don't appreciate the gifts God has given. Maybe we have a habit of fault-finding or a perfectionist streak that makes everything around us look wonky. As a result, we grow discontent with our jobs, families, husband, church, pastor, and even the very work of God in our lives.

When discontent, we feel the need to justify our murmuring with excuses. Some say, "My condition causes me to complain and be discontent." Really? When did God's grace become insufficient? Other Christians have risen about their conditions; why would you believe God could not lift you out as well?

I've heard others say, "I just can't be close to God because of my condition." Or, "The Lord seems so far away when I'm hurting like this." To depart from God further because affliction has made you feel He is not there is foolish. You need to draw closer! You need His comfort and correction. Learn to be content in every situation.

Some might complain, "People have mistreated me. I have a reason for my complaint." Jesus was treated worse than ever we were, yet we don't see Him complaining. Besides, are you looking to please men or God? God is the one who orders your life and the lives of others. Leave men's actions to the Lord. Answer for your own – your reaction is your choice! Blaming is a bad habit.

Another excuse is, "I never thought anything like this would happen to me." In Acts 20:22, 23, Paul lived expecting afflictions. They are a part of this sinful world. But, as Burroughs says, "With unexpected affliction comes unexpected mercy!" God is still there, no matter what surprise is around the corner. There is no need to complain – look to see Him at work around you.

And another one? "My problem is more significant or worse than everyone else." Burroughs cuts no slack here, saying, "Your problem/affliction is never greater than your sin. It is never worse than Hell. Your unsound heart makes it hurt worse. Your murmuring and discontent heighten your feelings. Your eye is evil to believe God is more gracious to others. He is no respecter of persons but loves all equally."

Then, some will say, "If I was experiencing some other affliction, I could bear it." What? We don't get to choose the methods of God. Besides, if we had other issues to deal with, it would not produce God's intention. We would still be murmuring if that is our mindset. We must learn to manage our ship no matter the wind. God chooses our path according to His purpose and will. We submit.

You know, we can moan and moan and moan, can't we? We think up numerous scenarios and excuses when we are disgruntled, murmuring, and discontent. We wrestle with God, and we run from the conviction of the Spirit. We blame others and become difficult and contrary. Envy and bitterness grow in our hearts, yet we think no one can smell our stink. But they can! It comes out in our words, facial expressions, reactions, and even opinions. But we hang on for dear life because we are too proud to admit we have a problem – we are a murmurer. We are discontent.

Dear friend, you can't hide it. God already sees it, hears it, and smells it. And even if you believe you have hidden it from others, it will break forth because what is in your heart must come out! It will not come out as a sweet, inward, quiet, gracious spirit submitting and delighting in God's will. Instead, it will burst forth in all its ugliness, damage your testimony, marriage, and working relationships, and leave you empty.

Burroughs says, "Murmuring is a disorder that lodges in men. Where it gets in once, it lodges, abides, and continues. We must dislodge it and get it out." The place to start is on your knees, confessing your sin of discontent and your murmuring spirit.

How then do we get to a place of contentment? Let's just say this plainly. We must set a good attitude in our hearts and repent of our discontented and murmuring spirit by asking God to change and renew. Nothing outside you can keep your heart in a good temper, it comes from within. Grace within your soul toward others and submission to God's sovereignty in all things tempers our hearts. We are where we are, and life is what it is. Settle this with God and be content. Start there, asking Him to forgive you for the stinky sin of discontentment.

Be content with what you have. Enjoy it. It is the gift of God. Release yourself from keeping up with the Jones's. Stop comparing yourself or your life with others. Make good with what you have and let God bring you more. Remember, stuff is temporary!

You've heard this before but let me remind you to count your blessings and let thankfulness and praise rise. Be serviceable to others and God. Get yourself back in line—Jesus and others and you, what a wonderful way to spell Joy. Loving service, restful hospitality, and acceptance of others express the spice of contentment. There's a calmness and beauty; there with a sweet-smelling savor.

Exercise faith. Psalm 27:13, "I had fainted, unless I had believed to see the goodness of the Lord in the land of the living." Burroughs puts it this way. "When reason can go no higher, let faith get on the shoulders of reason and say, 'I see land though reason cannot see it. I see good that will come out of all this evil.'" Why? Because the just live by faith!

Exercise your spiritual thinking. Meditate on heavenly things, pray, study, sing, memorize scripture, control your thoughts, and be thankful in everything. Interpret God's ways toward you as good. He is not a hard master but a good, good Father who desires loving, obedience, thankful, contented children.

I feel this has been a lot of focus on the stinkiness of murmuring and discontent. It is the ugly side of the spice. I hope it stinks to you. I know it stinks when I smell the smoke of discontentment in my home.

Contentment adds beautiful adjectives to our lives. "But the wisdom that is from above is first pure, then peaceable, gentle, and easy to be intreated, full of mercy and good fruits, without partiality, and without hypocrisy. And the fruit of righteousness is sown in peace of them that make peace" (James 3:17,18). That's what I want for my home and my life. What about you?

And Proverbs 24:3, 4 uses more beautiful descriptions that only come by use of the spice of contentment. "Though wisdom is an house builded; and by understanding it is established: and by knowledge shall the chambers be filled with all precious and pleasant riches." Do you want a happy life? Then make sure this spice of contentment is central to your home.

Dear friend, to be content you must make peace with God, peace with yourself, peace with others, and peace with your situation. "In everything give thanks, for this is the will of God in Christ Jesus concerning you" (1 Thessalonians 5:18). Be content with such things as ye have because contentment with godliness is great gain

53

(Hebrews 13:5; 1 Timothy 6:6), and it smells terrific!

You may want to read more about contentment and especially about the dangers of a murmuring spirit. In that case, Jeremiah Burrough's book – The Rare Jewel of Christian Contentment is free as a PDF on www.preachtheword.com. It's about 142 pages and packed full of thought and challenge. It is the best book I have ever read on contentment.

I pray the beautiful fragrance of contentment fills your life, and there is no smell of smoke left hanging around.

## For thought:

Are you guilty of murmuring and complaining as a perpetual habit?
Do you smell the smoke of discontent in your life?
How would your home smell if contentment was the fragrance?

## Scriptures to consider:

Philippians 4:11
1 Timothy 6:6, 17
Philippians 2:13-16

# THE SPICE OF PERSEVERANCE

Keep on Keeping On

Do you have any of those tried-and-true recipes? Those go-to dishes when company comes or comfort food the family raves over? Do you have some you can make with your eyes blindfolded, the ones you do when you are too tired or too distracted to think of anything else? We all need these.

It seems one of the most frequent decisions we make is what's for supper. I find it most annoying. I'm not a food lover, so I can have a slice of bread and butter and be just fine, but my husband is the opposite. So, persevering in the kitchen is one of my life challenges.

But persevering in life is a spice that demands more than a simple decision between beef or chicken. It is a must. You can skip a meal or two, but when you fail to persevere, there are consequences and a gnawing that eats away at your inner peace.

Perseverance has been necessary through this pandemic. And that's not all. Countries are wrangling and facing politics that divide and threaten war. It will take a sound mind and a steady heart to continue forward. But continue, we must.

Some people put their heads down during times like these and push through. Others let anger overtake them, while some fall back in their beds and take a long time to rise again.

As I thought about what the right attitude would be, the Christian attitude in the face of hard times and the need for perseverance, I found those reactions don't match with Christ's example.

Coming to earth in the form of a man, laying aside His power, and submitting to human limitations was indeed an exercise in perseverance for Christ. But we don't see Jesus doggedly pushing through, reacting in anger, or falling into self-pity. And even the Apostle Paul talks about being bound in an earthly body, which limited his spiritual desires. Yet, he, too, did not approach ministry and life in these ways.

So, why do we? Well, I think it is because we have learned to push through. Haven't we? To keep on keeping on. And there is a proper element of that attitude in the spice of perseverance. Isaiah 50:7, speaking of Jesus, says he "set his face like a flint." Jesus worked with determination toward a goal, but he wasn't stubborn or pushing through to prove His point. Instead, His perseverance was about attaining His God-given purpose—the salvation of our souls, the fulfilling of God's will.

But our pushing through is usually based on the power of self – our will. We keep on because we want something or are determined not to lose. We fear failure and want to control our world, so we pull the reins tighter and hunker down.

Our anger reveals our inner frustration at not being able to control our world. So we lash out at those in our way, irritated by the limitations we face. The poor person behind the cash register or the kid in the drive-thru window gets our spite and verbal unkindness because we have chosen anger as our path. This is our way of persevering and woe be to anyone who gets in our way.

And when we fall back into our bed, pulling the covers over our head, our lack of perseverance takes another dangerous turn. Depression and self-pity take over, and we find ourselves staying too long in our pit. Everything looks hard, confusing, and too bleak to face. We start hearing inner thoughts like, "It will never be the same. It will always be like this." Remember, the words never and always indicate a lie is nearby. Negative thinking hammers nails into our coffin as we pine away. That isn't perseverance. That is pouting.

Okay, so how do we activate this spice of perseverance instead of doggedly pushing through, giving way to anger, or falling into self-pity? I think you'll be surprised by the actual way you appropriate this spice. It is called surrender! We persevere by adding the spice of surrender.

Again, let's go back to Jesus' example. He didn't just push through, act with anger, or feel sorry for His plight. Instead, He surrendered His will to the will of the Father. As He faced the cross, the most pivotal point in His mission, look at His responses at Gethsemane. He sweats drops of blood in prayer as He draws aside to gain strength and comes to the final surrender – "nevertheless, thy will be done." Surrender gave Jesus perseverance and strength to endure the crucifixion.

And when you look at the Apostle Paul, you see his attitude – he left everything behind and pressed forth; not with a will of determination, but with a surrender of all that was of value in this world that he might win Christ and be found in Him. It was this surrender that allowed him to face the beatings and stoning and even to be willing to go to Rome, knowing it would most likely cost him his life. He did these things willingly. He could persevere because he had already surrendered everything to the Lord.

Maybe we need to stop just a moment and think about what the spice of surrender means? This isn't the type of surrender where you wave a white flag and give everything you have over to an enemy. It isn't a surrender that makes you an unworthy servant or cast away. It isn't surrendering to failure. No. It is the total opposite. And I think this is the most beautiful thing about surrender – it has properties of richness and blessing that cannot come from any other spice.

When we surrender and wave our white flag to Christ, it isn't losing; it's winning. We win Christ, a home in Heaven, and the salvation of our soul. So then, as we further surrender our life, thoughts, motives, and yes, every part of our being, we win! With each surrender, we gain strength, purpose, and fulfilment.

When we surrender, we aren't losing all our belongings; we are being filled with all heavenly blessings. All the riches of Heaven become ours when we are adopted and made friends with God. We win.

When we surrender, we don't become an unworthy servant or a cast away. We are engrafted into the vine. We become vessels fit for the Master's use. We become bond-servants - one in love with their Master and share all the benefits of the family. We win. So how do we apply that to our current situation? Here's how I see it.

I can moan and whine about everything going on. I can allow anger and frustration to rise in my heart. I can push through with an inner tightness. Or I can relax and remember God is in control. My times are in His hands. I know He fulfills all His promises and will not fail. My circumstances do not deter God's promise. My faith can rest. I can breathe easy.

I can use this time to examine the anger and self-pity in my heart and surrender those weaknesses to Him. If I do, I will come through this test much stronger and better equipped for the challenges ahead. And there is more to come! We will need all the strength and perseverance surrender can muster for the pandemic and the politics.

Just yesterday, as I read my Bible reading, God brought more of the truth of perseverance to my heart. Read these portions from Hebrews 6.

Verses 10-11 reads, "For God is not unrighteous to forget your work and labour of love, which ye have shewed toward his name, in that ye have ministered to the saints, and do minister. And we desire that every one of you do shew the same diligence to the full assurance of hope unto the end."

Persevere. God knows your good works. He sees your efforts of love, so have diligence and assurance and hope. Diligence means eagerness, zeal, and has the idea of doing it without delay.

Assurance means conviction and certainty. Hope means with expectation—what a beautiful description of perseverance. There is action, conviction, and an expected outcome.

Verse 15 reads, "And so, after he (Abraham) had patiently endured, he obtained the promise." The blessing we seek, the hope before us, comes after we patiently endure. The blessing is on the other side of obedience – and perseverance!

I think you'll like the definition of endure. It means to exhibit internal and external control in difficult circumstances and suffer long. This pandemic and political circus demand a measure of internal and external control, don't they? We are being required to suffer long, be patient, and endure to the end! And the end will come.

Verse 19 says, "Which hope we have as an anchor of the soul, both sure and steadfast." We have this hope in us – the hope of salvation, the hope of God's return. This world is not our home, our souls are anchored in Jesus, and we can endure because our anchor is sure and steadfast, meaning firm and binding, certain, definite.

Perseverance then is not dogged determination; it is a mindset upon the expectation of God's purpose and surrendered to that purpose. Ephesians 1:11, "He does all things according to the purpose of His will." We can surrender to that!

It isn't living life in fear because of circumstances. It is looking beyond the pressures of today to the promise that is sure, firm, and binding with hope and assurance.

And it leaves no room for wailing upon our beds because there is a pressing urgency to our activity. We are to be about our Father's business, patiently persevering to the end.

Hebrews 10:35, 36 reads, "Cast not away therefore your confidence which hath great recompense of reward." (In other words, don't give up!) "For ye have need of patience (perseverance) that, after ye have done the will of God, ye might receive the promise."

And what is that promise? Revelation 2:10 tells us "Fear none of those things which thou shalt suffer...be thou faithful unto death, and I will give thee a crown of life." We win through perseverance and surrender. So, let's patiently and consistently press on with determination, zeal, and hope to the end and surrender the rest to God!

**For thought:**

What describes your attitude toward the challenges of today?
Are you guilty of dogged determination, crying in your bed, or living in fear?
How does perseverance give us strength?

**Scriptures to consider:**

Psalm 119:49
Proverbs 16:3
1 Peter 4:12, 13

# THE SPICE OF OBEDIENCE

Hear and Do

The spice of obedience. It is the first one we learn as children. And though it is elementary, we spend most of our lives struggling with obedience. Our intense desire for our own way and the autonomy of our sinful heart puts up barriers toward our parents, teachers, rules of the road, tax laws, staying on a diet, and toward the Lord.

The book of James breaks this spice down into two words – hear and do. James 1:22-25 reads. "But be ye doers of the word, and not hearers only, deceiving your own selves. For if any be a hearer of the word, and not a doer, he is like unto a man beholding his natural face in a glass: For he beholdeth himself, and goeth his way, and straightway forgetteth what manner of man he was."

Can you see the two words? Hear and do. It's a simple command, so why do we struggle?

I don't know about you, but as a young Christian, I found some of the things the preacher preached, or I read in Christian books, hard to accept and understand. The conversation of my new Christian friends didn't make sense or sometimes seemed extreme and odd. I wondered how others grew in the Lord and feared I might be left behind. I even found some of what I read in the Bible hard to accept. Like tithing, for example. Why should I give ten percent of my income? My dad always put a dollar in the offering plate. That seemed fine to me. Forgiveness? Am I to forgive even when the other person hasn't asked or made amends? Love? Am I to love those that don't treat me nice? How do I do that? Anger? I'm not to be angry? I'm to learn to control my tongue and attitude, even when others don't? That seemed a bit unfair.

We face many questions as we grow and learn in our Christian lives. But these two words form the basis of obedience. So, let's see if we can understand what God is telling us.

Proverbs 3:5 says, "Trust in the Lord with all thine heart; and lean not unto thine own understanding." One of the most significant challenges we face is the hurdle of our own understanding. God created us with an intellect, and we should use it, but sometimes our mind begins thinking it is more powerful, more intelligent, and greater than its Creator.

God often warns us about this type of pride. For example, in Proverbs 3:7, He repeats almost the exact idea as 3:5 – "Be not wise in thine own eyes."

Sometimes we have baggage, misconceptions, or hold certain prejudices that buck against what God's word teaches, and we struggle to bring them in line with Scripture. We think we are right because we have always believed a particular way and find it hard to change.

Not long into my Christian walk, I found a verse in Proverbs that helped me with this. Proverbs 21:30 says, "There is no wisdom nor understanding nor counsel against the Lord."

This one verse still helps me when my mind wants to figure things out. I recite that verse, and then I agree with God that His wisdom is correct. If He says something is good, there is a particular way to do something or an attitude I need to adapt; I submit, stop trying to figure it out, and simply act by faith. God is always right, and I need to stop fighting against Him. There is no way to win! "There is no wisdom nor understanding nor counsel against the Lord." That is what hearing and doing is all about.

You will struggle to "do" if you disagree with what you are "hearing," right? So, the first thing you must establish in your heart is that the Word you have before you – God's Word – is right. It is the correct way to do things. It holds the proper perspective on life and promises the best outcome. Then, you take your questions through the Word and discover what you should do.

Let me give you an example. In the book of Luke, we find the disciples out fishing. Remember, these guys are experienced, professional fishermen. They had toiled all night and caught nothing. Jesus comes by and asks them to put the ship out again so He can use it to teach the people. So, they did. They heard and did.

When Jesus finished, He told Simon to throw out the nets again. Simon's answer is what would most likely be ours as well. "Jesus," Simon says, "We worked all night at this and caught nothing! We are professional fishermen. But, if you say so, I hear you! I'll do it! I'll let down the nets again." This time, they caught so many fish their net broke.

They heard and did, based on what the Lord told them. That is the key – obedience based on His word. Remember, Jesus was not a fisherman. He was a carpenter. What did He know about fishing? They were the professionals; they were the ones with the experience. They knew what to do, but they yielded and obeyed the Lord of creation, who knew exactly where the fish were!

Sometimes we take a similar attitude with things we hear from the pulpit or read in our Bible. Our experience, understanding, and opinion are where we place our faith – where we make our decisions. We aren't willing to hear, much less obey. And when we fail to hear or block what we hear by our own opinion or ideas, we are guilty of stubbornness and rebellion. We are quenching and grieving the Holy Spirit and trying to make sense of God's Word by our own intellect.

But God isn't impressed with our ideas. He doesn't need our opinion. He wants us to yield and obey. Remember Proverbs 21:30? "There is no wisdom nor understanding nor counsel against the Lord."

God's opinions are much bigger and better. His have an intent of blessing, and He knows how to make it happen! We are to trust and obey. Do you know that song? "Trust and obey, for there's no other way to be happy in Jesus, but to trust and obey." It's another simple truth but so full of promise.

Hebrews 11:6 tells us it is impossible to please God without faith. Our faith is exhibited by accepting and faithfully doing what the Word of God says. It isn't about smarts or opinions but wholehearted obedience.

The Bible gives other examples of people who cast away their earthly understanding and stepped out by faith to obey; to hear and do what God had shown them.

Rahab heard about the God of the Israelites. So, she hid the spies, and God saved her and her family.

Abraham heard God calling him to leave home, so he went out, not knowing where he was to go, and God gave him a land, a son, and a nation.

Gideon heard God calling him to become the man to lead the army and, even though he was unsteady at first, he obeyed. And God used him to break Israel free from their enemy.

The woman with the pots. I love this story. The poor woman's husband died and left her with two sons and heavy financial debt. The prophet told her to gather pots from all her neighbors. I'm sure that seemed odd, but she and her sons collected as many vessels as they could, and God filled them with enough oil to pay her debt and live off the rest.

Sometimes, obedience is challenging, but we can be sure God will keep His promise if we follow on by faith.

Let's look at hearing and doing another way. We are to live by faith, by the same faith that brought us to Christ. You heard the word of salvation, and what did you do? You came to Christ, confessing your need of a Saviour and asking His forgiveness. And how did God bless? He forgave your sins and made you anew.

If you haven't yet done that, Romans 10:17 tells us, "Faith cometh by hearing." First, we hear the word of God. Then, in Romans 10:9, we do something about it. You confess with your mouth and believe in your heart. That is the doing part. And what does God promise will happen? Romans 10:13, "Whosoever shall call upon the name of the Lord shall be saved." Accepting Christ is the first step of hearing and doing. Then, as you learn to walk this new life in Christ, you succeed by doing the same thing – following the same pattern – hearing and doing.

When you hear something from God's word, whether it is baptism, tithing, giving, helping others, speaking for Christ, loving, forgiving, or whatever it might be. When you hear it – do it! Do it by faith, and God will bless. We live by the same faith that brought us to Christ based on His Word, His promises, and His ability. Hear and do.

So, what has the Lord been speaking to you about lately? Where do you need to obey? You will find it always matches His Word, and He will keep placing it on your heart and in your ears until you obey. It will challenge you to cast out your net!

The blessing is on the other side of obedience. John Greenleaf Whittier wrote, "Nothing before, nothing behind, the steps of faith fall on the seeming void, and find the rock beneath."

Stepping out and walking by faith is not a blind walk; it is a confident, assured stride based on the knowledge of God's word, character, and promises, but you will never know what it is like until you step out in obedience. Then, you will find Him waiting for you there.

So, let me encourage you. Hear – listen to what the Lord says, to His word, to the preacher, and do. Obey what the Bible instructs. Take each step by faith, and you will grow and find yourself in the place of blessing.

Revelation 1:3 – "Blessed is he that readeth, and they that hear the words of this prophecy, and keep those things which are written therein: for the time is at hand."

There are those two keywords again - they that hear and they that keep or do! Two workable words to take you forward, grow your faith, and position you for God's blessings.

The spice of obedience is very simple – hear and do!

## For thought:

Do you struggle with obedience?
How less complicated would life be if you worked from simply hearing and doing?
What blessing might be waiting for you on the other side of obedience?

## Scriptures to consider:

1 Peter 5:5, 6
Proverbs 19::21
Proverbs 14:12

# THE SPICE OF GRATITUDE

Thankfulness

Thanksgiving is a very deliberate and punctuated spice. God places it in prominence, saying, "In everything give thanks, for this is the will of God in Christ Jesus concerning you" (1 Thessalonians 5:18). In everything. The more I practice thankfulness, the more thankful I become because I experience the truth of Romans 8:28, that all things do work together for good.

When we come to the spice of thanksgiving or gratitude, we must face the fact that sometimes it can be hard to find. Sometimes the things happening around us, the things we feel are missing, or the expectations we have created do not arouse a thankful spirit.

Thanksgiving is about seeing God's goodness in every circumstance and every moment. God is perpetually good, providing and caring for us daily. We can be thankful for His consistency no matter our situation.

Much like contentment, thankfulness is a spice that creates a warming aroma. It makes everything else more tasteful. Take this pandemic – since that is happening at the time of this writing. It seems such an odd place to be. But if we can find our way to adopt an attitude of thankfulness even in these times, we will experience several benefits – benefits that will help carry us through.

Thankfulness reduces depression and negative emotions such as envy, hate, and anger. It increases our energy level and productivity making us feel better about ourselves and helping us reduce and cope with negative stress. In addition, thankful people sleep better, have more robust immune systems, and have better blood pressure. Thankful people have deeper friendships, are friendlier, reach goals faster, and have increased feelings of happiness and well-being.

Max Lucado said, "A grateful heart sees each day as a gift. Thankful people focus less on what they lack and more on the privileges they have. A grateful heart is like a magnet sweeping over the day, collecting reasons for gratitude."

Have you ever felt like that? Like everything you saw in your life made you even more thankful. The stars in the sky, the eyes with which you read, the lungs that inhale and exhale eleven thousand liters of air every day. For the jam on your toast, the blanket that warms you, and the comfy bed at night. For the smiles of those around you and the children around your table. Everything around you exudes a beautiful glow of the gift of God.

It reminds me of James 1:17 – "Every good gift and every perfect gift is from above, and cometh down from the father of lights, with whom is no variableness, neither shadow of turning." Everything we have is a gift from God – a good gift. Therefore, we should allow our hearts to count our blessings and live in an attitude of gratefulness.

"Gratitude," Max Lucado says, "gets us through the hard stuff. Gratitude always leaves us looking at God and away from dread. It does to anxiety what the morning sun does to valley mist. It burns it up." We can't stay long in the valley of anxiety when we acknowledge all God's accomplishments and provision with a heart of thankfulness.

I think gratitude or an attitude of thankfulness is always a choice. We can't control circumstances, but we can control our reactions. We can learn to see the sun through the fog. Even in this time of restriction and pandemic, we can look and see God at work. Let's think about some of the things we have seen coming out of our situation.

People are showing teamwork by caring for the ill and finding a cure as we have a common problem. People are being more innovative by changing and adapting their businesses, schooling, and a host of other ways to protect others. Kindness and love are shown through community support, volunteers, and genuine kindness as they look after elderly and vulnerable neighbours.

Chuck Swindoll said, "Life is 10% what happens to you and 90% how you react to it." So if I have the choice of how I want to react to this pandemic, then I choose to respond with gratitude. That gives me a 90% chance of success.

I plan to sit down, make a list of things I am thankful for, and share those blessings with others. I want to meditate this week on thankfulness and allow that spice to permeate my thoughts. Then, I want to share it. To write a note or make a call or send a text expressing my thankfulness for someone or maybe several someones! I want to keep that spark – that spice of thanksgiving – alive in my heart and my home, for this is the will of God in Christ Jesus concerning me, and concerning you.

Not long ago, I came across a TedTalk by David Steindl-Rast entitled, Want to be happy? Be grateful. As I listened, I saw other benefits and sides of this spice. He says, "There is something that we know about everyone we meet anywhere in the world that is the very mainspring of whatever they do and whatever they put up with. And that is that all of us want to be happy. In this, we are all together. How we imagine our happiness, that differs from one another, but it's already a lot that we have all in common, that we want to be happy."

Have you ever equated thankfulness with happiness? Can you imagine having one without the other? I can't. He goes on to make this distinction, "It is not happiness that makes us grateful. It's gratefulness that makes us happy." So, thankfulness/gratefulness ordered by God is more than a command. It is a blessing in disguise. It is a channel to our happiness.

He explains that gratefulness cannot be solely an occasional experience. It must become a way of living. And how do we do that? "By experiencing," He says, "by becoming aware that every moment is a given moment. It's a gift. You haven't earned it. You haven't brought it about in any way. You have no way of assuring that there will be another moment given to you, and yet, that's the most valuable thing that can ever be given to us, this moment, with all the opportunity that it contains. If we didn't have this present moment, we wouldn't have any opportunity to do anything or experience anything, and this moment is a gift. We can avail ourselves of this opportunity, or we can miss it, and if we avail ourselves of the opportunity, it is the key to happiness. Behold the master key to our happiness in our own hands. Moment by moment, we can be grateful for this gift."

I began looking at what I was doing with the moments given me. Am I using them wisely? Am I thankful for each moment? Do I realize the fleet-fulness of life and seize each moment with a grateful and expectant heart?

Then, he began addressing the question so many have asked. Must I be thankful for everything that has happened to me?

He says, "Does that mean that we can be grateful for everything? Certainly not. We cannot be grateful for violence, for war, for oppression, for exploitation. On the personal level, we cannot be grateful for the loss of a friend, for unfaithfulness, for bereavement. But I didn't say we can be grateful for everything. I said we can be grateful in every given moment for the opportunity, and even when we are confronted with something that is terribly difficult, we can rise to this occasion and respond to the opportunity that is given to us."

Do you see how he brought it back to the spice of gratitude? Sure, bad things happen, but still, our attitude is critical. Keeping things in the proper perspective creates a broader avenue of thankfulness for us. In everything, God is there. He alone can turn ashes into beauty. We can be thankful for that!

He continues, "Once in a while, something very difficult is given to us, and when this difficult thing occurs, it's a challenge to rise to that opportunity, and we can rise to it by learning something which is sometimes painful. Learning patience, for instance. We have been told that the road to peace is not a sprint, but is more like a marathon. That takes patience. That's difficult. It may be to stand up for your opinion, to stand up for your conviction. That's an opportunity that is given to us. To learn, to suffer, to stand up, all these opportunities are given to us, but they are opportunities, and those who avail themselves of those opportunities are the ones that we admire. They make something out of life."

I think this is the real challenge of gratitude: looking beyond the difficulty to the opportunity. Sometimes, we get knocked down by a hard spot in the road and fail to look beyond the mud in our face. We believe we will never recover, but the opportunity to pick ourselves up and continue forward is there if we take hold of this spice of thankfulness. God is the God of second chances, and thankfully, forgiveness and restoration are His specialties.

So how do we apply this spice to our lives? How do we learn to live in thanksgiving and gratitude? I see it as a daily choice, an attitude that guides my day. That adage of counting your blessings works!

The speaker caught my attention when he began pointing out the benefits of gratitude. He said, "It can change our world in immensely important ways, because if you're grateful, you're not fearful, and if you're not fearful, you're not violent. If you're grateful, you act out of a sense of enough and not of a sense of scarcity, and you are willing to share. If you are grateful, you are enjoying the differences between people, and you are respectful to everybody, and that changes this power pyramid under which we live. And it doesn't make for equality, but it makes for equal respect, and that is the important thing."

Such is the effect of thankfulness on our lives and the lives of those around us. "Grateful people are joyful people," the speaker concluded. And I would have to agree.

So, as you consider your gratitude quotient, how grateful are you for what God has given? What attitude guides your life and responses? Can you see that thankfulness is an incense that rises alongside contentment? Are you willing to obey God's command and develop a deeper appreciation for the spice of thankfulness?

I hope so, for thankful people are happy people, and I believe the love of Christ is shown best through those with a high ratio of thankfulness.

**For thought:**

How thankful are you?
Are there areas in your life that still need to be flavored with gratitude?
If thankful people are happy people, how happy are you?


**Scriptures to consider:**

Psalm 68:19
Psalm 34:1-3
Colossians 3:15

# THE SPICE OF SERVICE

Can I Serve You?

So far, we have looked at prayer, meditation, study, waiting, simplicity, stillness, contentment, perseverance, surrender, obedience, and thankfulness. That is by no means an exhaustive list of things God wants us to add to our lives, but it does make for enough challenge! Today, we are going to talk about the spice of service.

You see, spices are of no use left sitting on a shelf; you have to pull them out and use them. Service is where we use our spices – where people see what has been happening within us as we pray, meditate, study, and develop our inner qualities. Service reveals our attitude and spiritual maturity. It is the giving out of what has been taking place inwardly.

I'm reminded of Jeremiah's comment in Jeremiah 20:9, "But his word was in mine heart as a burning fire shut up in my bones." What the Lord had planted in his heart had to come out! And when we spend time in prayer, study, and meditation, God fills our hearts with the heat of His Word. It must come out. And it is usually seen in service. Serving is love in action developed from a loving, sincere relationship with God.

On the night Jesus was being betrayed, He took a towel and girded Himself, giving us the ultimate example of service as He washed the feet of the disciples. His heart was full. Knowing what was ahead, He looked around at the men for whom He was about to give His life. They had walked alongside Him, been tutored by Him, and sat, seemingly ignorant of what was about to take place. Yet, in love, Jesus humbled Himself and served them.

With the washing complete, Jesus basically said, "Do you understand what I have done? You call me Lord, and that's who I am. So, if I am your Lord and I have washed your feet, you should also wash one another's feet." He is showing them the importance of serving others. (John 13:13, 14)

And a little while later, Jesus tells them, "By this shall all men know that ye are my disciples, if ye have love one to another" (John 13:35), and Galatians 5:13 says, "By love, serve one another." This is the reason behind service – love for others – the second commandment, right? Love God with all your heart and your neighbor as yourself.

Jesus served the disciples and others. He took the opportunity to reach out and give His virtue or goodness to those around him. Luke 6:35 tells us, "He was kind to the unthankful and to the evil." He is our example.

He didn't distinguish the small from the large, the deserving or undeserving. He didn't calculate the results. He ministered simply and faithfully to everyone because He loved them and saw their need. He knew his calling – to be about His Father's business, which motivated His service.

Service is a gift of the Spirit, and I am so thankful for the people in our church and people I have met who have this gift. It is so precious and refreshing to see people willing to build the family, church, and community. Where would we be without the people who are willing to put hands and feet to their prayers? But service is a spice we are all called to use. Romans 12:1 calls us to our reasonable service.

To serve well, we need to understand a servant's attitude. A good servant knows whom he serves. Colossians 3:24 says, "ye serve the Lord Christ." Service isn't about a personal agenda or people-pleasing; it is about honoring Christ. It is vital to keep this one-mindedness at the forefront. We serve Christ.

A good servant doesn't promote his own ideas or opinions. Instead, he honors and obeys God's Word because he knows God's way is best, and any reward he would ever have comes by obedience and from God's hand alone.

A good servant accepts God's supremacy in all things. He knows his place and is willing to wait on the Lord's timing. He can withhold service as freely as he performs it. He can serve by waiting in silence because he wisely knows he is seeking God's timing, not his own. That's because the excellent servant has another spice deep in his heart – the spice of humility.

Humility is one of those virtues that develops in hiddenness. Thinking we have it is sure evidence that we don't. Humility isn't something that falls to us. It is a quality we seek and refine by submission to God's will. It's like grace that grows more beautiful with age. The humblest people I know would be embarrassed if I told them they were humble and would think they had acted out of place if I noticed their humility.

Humble people serve. They put the needs of others first and consistently seek to be a blessing. Service is conducive to the growth of humility because when we serve with the right motive and with our focus on blessing others, a deep change occurs in our spirits.

Jesus even took time to talk about the right attitude of service in the Sermon on the Mount. It seems the Pharisees and religious leaders loved to make a show of their service by sounding trumpets as they gave their alms. Still, just as Jesus said to shut the door in prayer, he also says our alms (our service and giving) should be secret. And then, God will reward openly.

He says, "When thou doest alms, let not thy left hand know what thy right hand doeth" (Matthew 6:3). Alms are when you help someone with gifts, handouts, or assistance. It's not just money in the plate. It is meeting the need of another – serving them tangibly, but without show.

Maybe we need to talk about different types of service. Sometimes we get the idea that service is like waiting tables or doing the dirty work. But it is much more than that.

Service can be sharing your testimony with someone. You serve others as you pray for them or when you help them bear burdens. You serve by teaching and even preaching because you are giving something God has given you to others.

You can serve by listening, showing common courtesy, and giving hospitality, offering that cup of cold water in the name of the Lord.

You serve when you guard the reputation of others by stopping gossip and even when you gracefully receive service – allowing others to give, help, or serve you. You serve by gracious acceptance.

And service can be those little things you must constantly do – cooking, cleaning, going to work, all those everyday things we do to make our house a home and keep body and soul together. We can do them with the same love Jesus showed in washing His disciples' feet. It just comes down to our attitude. You see, if we are humble servants, no service is beneath us. We willingly do all things heartily as unto the Lord.

In Luke 17, Jesus is talking to the disciples about a man with a servant, saying, "but which of you, having a servant plowing or feeding cattle, will say unto him by and by, when he is come from the field, Go and sit down to meat? And will not rather say unto him, Make ready wherewith I may sup, and gird thyself, and serve me, till I have eaten and drunken; and afterward thou shalt eat and drink? Doth he thank that servant because he did the things that were commanded him? To trow not." ("I don't think so," Jesus said.) "So, likewise ye, when he shall have done all those things which are commanded you, say, We are unprofitable servants: we have done that which was our duty to do."

I like that passage. It reminds me of Romans 12:1, 2. What we do for the Lord and others is our "reasonable service."

Do you see what Jesus is saying? The servant did his work in the field, but his next job was to work for the master – waiting on him that evening. There was no earning of thanks, only an expectation of duty and obedience between master and servant.

When it comes to our service and the example of Christ, it is the same. We are to be about our Father's business. We are not sent to be ministered to but to minister, following Christ's example. And when we have done our duty, we have not made God our debtor. We have done our reasonable service. And that service is profitable because "God is not unrighteous to forget your labour of love, which ye have shewed toward his name, in that ye have ministered and do minister" (Hebrews 6:10). God sees our service, and He sees how we do it.

So, maybe we need to be thinking about our manner of service. Are we waiting for a big thank you and some applause? Do we see ourselves as grander because we have done a good deed? Can we be content if no one knows what we did. Can we serve in secret and let the Lord reward us? Are we doing our service as unto the Lord? Or are we seeking to please others or serving for recognition? Arc we serving heartily – giving all we can without a selfish goal? Are we gracious or bossy? Willing or difficult?

This spice of service has a way of revealing our true motives and spiritual immaturity. Service will be like a burr under our saddle if our attitude is wrong. We will feel resentful, uncomfortable, and an atmosphere of murmuring will start, and others will smell it! We've talked about that before, haven't we?

One more thought I had about service is that service is creative. It looks to see the need and then finds ways to meet it.

This past week a lady told me she was growing frustrated with the limitations placed on their ministry due to Covid19. She was concerned to be only able to keep contact with their people by telephone, no face-to-face visits, no church services, no group fellowships. I had to agree that we are experiencing ministry challenges. "How can we serve if we can't get out there," she asked?

That's where creativity comes in. Thankfully, we still have telephone, internet, and social media to help us keep in contact with others and serve them through live streaming, videos, zoom, and a host of other avenues. I know this pandemic has pushed our church to be more creative. We are serving even more people now through our online preaching and teaching. And that's a good thing.

I've watched missionaries pushing creativity in children's ministries. For example, one had a socially distanced picnic in the park. Each family brought their own food, and the missionary had socially distanced hula-hoops collectively in one area. Each family sat within their personal hula-hoop. They ate their picnic, talked, and even played some socially distanced games as a group. That's creative, I think!

This same missionary arranged a church walk. Because there were several elderly living within a walking distance of the church, family groups were spaced at timed intervals. They walked a pre-set path passing the homes of each elderly resident who sat on their front lawn, where the children picked up a different bag placed on a table or the front walk at each home.

One bag contained a book, another a sweet, another a small toy. The kids had a great time. The elderly participated, meeting their loneliness, and everyone safely saw each other.

I heard of another church that held a live stream Vacation Bible School, and they posted out to each child a complete set of crafts, handouts, and trinkets.

You've probably heard of loads more ideas than I have, but the point is, we don't have to allow restrictions to stop our service. We just need to be more creative.

People still love to get a phone call or a letter in the post. You can serve that way by including a few words of kindness, a bookmarker, or even a photo. Take time to be creative in the way you reach out. Create a prayer group through Facebook or

WhatsApp and meet regularly. Serve personably and purposefully. We all need encouragement.

"God is not unrighteous to forget your labour of love, which ye have shewed toward his name, in that ye have ministered to the saints, and do minister" (Hebrews 6:10).

Let's use the spices God has placed in our hearts and pour them out as a sweet-smelling savor. Then, by love, let's humbly serve one another.

**For thought:**

How's your service?
Have you allowed the challenges of the pandemic to hinder your service?
Do you wait for service that can be noticed or are you content to serve behind the scenes?

**Scriptures to consider:**

Psalm 100
1 Corinthians 3:6-9
2 Corinthians 10:18

# ABOUT THE AUTHOR

**GAIL GRITTS** has served the Lord as a church planting missionary in England for over 35 years alongside her husband, Tom.

While still active in church planting and ministry abroad, Gail is a blogger (Beside the Well), shares devotional lessons on YouTube, and is the author of five other devotional books, and a series of children's books called Reba and Katherine.

Find her blog at ggritts.blogspot.com, and more about her work and access her other devotional books from her website.

Connect with Gail

www.gailgritts.com

Facebook – Gail Gritts Author

# OTHER DEVOTIONAL WORKS

Anxious? Worried? Need help to keep perspective and some fuel for your relationships? Let's put some light on the subject!

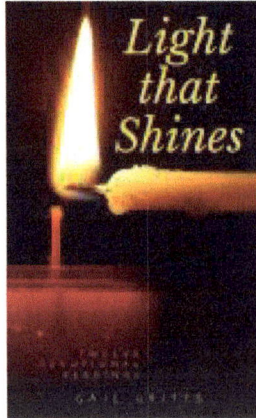

Many people still have feelings of captivity, fear, and confusion leaving them unsettled and discontent. Contentment and Captives gives pointers on coping, self-care, thriving, and maintaining strong mental health.

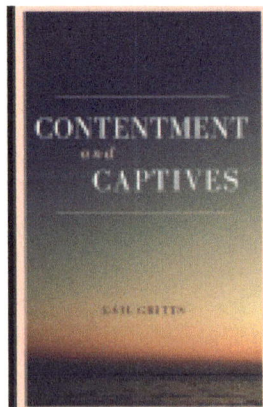

When depression leaves us torn down, it is refreshing to learn we can rebuild those walls of protection and strength. Build That Wall gives you Biblical tools for reinforcing your life.

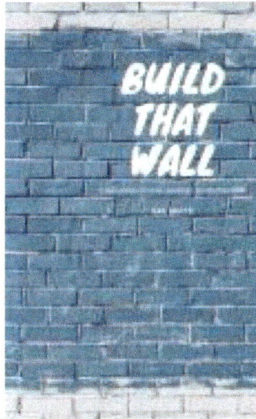

Grab a cup of tea, cuddle down in your favorite chairs, and let's talk about the things we are feeling, the place where we find ourselves, and remember God is still beside us. Let's visit.

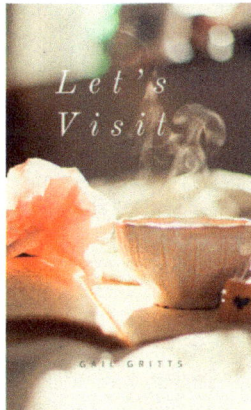

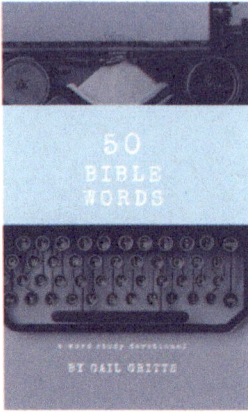

A devotional word study bringing application to everyday life that will feed your soul and expand your understanding. 50 Bible Words is a tool to direct your meditation and open a variety of windows of thought.

Made in the USA
Columbia, SC
22 June 2022

62007276R00055